They Speak Through Me
Messages From Beyond

by
Bob Buchanan

Cover design by Bob Buchanan
Author photo by Jessica Buchanan

Published by Volossal Publishing
www.volossal.com

Dedication

This book is dedicated to God and the Divine Spirits who have granted me these gifts. I'm thankful for the strength they give me to continue this journey and for allowing me to stay on this path helping others when I can. They give me the confidence I need whenever I waver and question myself and these gifts.

To all the Souls who come to me with messages for those they look over and care for. I thank them for guiding me, showing me the way to help others walk through their darkness to the light. Without them, my work and this book would not be possible. I thank them every day for their support.

It is to them I dedicate this book. It is to them I surrender, knowing they will never let me down.

Table of Contents

Foreward

It is an honor for me to have been asked to write the forward for this book. The first question one might ask is, "What is a Caul bearer?" I had never heard that term prior to meeting Bob Buchanan. I had experienced many psychics, astrologers and mediums throughout my life, but it wasn't until I met Bob for the first time, that I became quite intrigued at how accurate he was with messages from friends and family members that had passed.

So again, I wondered, **what is a Caul Bearer?**

"A caul bearer is a person who is born with the caul. The caul is also known as the "veil", the "hood", the "mantle", or the "veil of tears". What they see, hear, and feel, tells tales of things to come, things from the past, and things we all need to know. They are messengers who are in touch with the world beyond the physical plane. They are sensitives, visionaries, shamans, mediums, and healers. Writers, actors, poets, artists." 1

In essence, Caul bearers are often found to have been granted a special gift. This gift is one of knowing, understanding, healing and the ability to communicate messages from those who have passed to the other side of life, as we know it.

After years of denial and trying to hide from this gift, Bob realized that he was actually denying his calling - and denying the mission God set out for him. You see, Caul bearers, like Bob, use their intuitive abilities to see a person's past, present and immediate future events, by turning to the soul energies surrounding that person. Perhaps, to find wisdom, guidance or simply peace.

My personal experience with Bob has been enlightening and supportive through some very difficult times, over the last several years. Both professionally and personally, Bob has been able to show a path that makes sense to me by sharing messages from those who know me, who are now on the other side. Bob has been able to provide guidance and calm when I was confused or not sure of what to do with a specific situation. It has been extremely comforting to be able to hear the messages from loved ones who know me best and know how to truly guide me. Bob cares about people. He wants to help others, as he is selfless in his work. Bob has been the infinite messenger and for that, I am forever grateful.

Bob has been guided to tell the story of his life experiences by writing this book, He shares true stories of individuals whom he has been able to support through their times of grief, loss and pondering life's many challenges. Bob, has taken his gift to the fullest by helping others in their journey to find the truth, happiness and peace.

> \- Linda John
> October 2017

Notes:
1. http://whatisacaulbearer.webs.com/aboutcaulbearers.htm

Preface

Spiritual gifts and abilities have always been a part of me and my life. They've been an influence on my life although I never realized how much. I somehow always knew what was about to happen or what was coming; however, I was not able to fully grasp or understand this. It put the fear of God in me. Crazy feelings and visions that came to me for no reason, at any time, frightened me as a child. There was no one around to help me understand them. I was so scared I spent my life burying what was happening; running away from them and refusing to acknowledge them. I spoke with Medium Sheri Perback, the only person who saw I absolutely needed to do this. We had an argument while on the phone about me "coming out," as I called it. I told her it wasn't going to happen. She told me I had no choice. Sure enough, she was right.

I realize now that it was God and the Divine Spirits guiding me all along. The Divine Spirits surrounded and protected me from drowning, from being hit by bullets that were coming at me from enraged people, and from the blades thrust at me as a police officer.

It is only now I understand that my life has always been a journey toward accepting and being open to these gifts. It is only now I can see this as I look back. You will read more about how this journey took place, where it has taken me to date and how it has helped me.

I am very grateful and humbled by all that has happened to me over the past several years. All this comes from people who refer me. I'm in awe of the events that occur.

This journey is about spirituality, not religion. The Divine Spirits guide me through this life. They have never let me down. I trust, they never will.

Acknowledgements

My deepest appreciation goes out to my guardian angel here on earth, without her this book would not have been possible. Thank you, Carolyn Farley

My heartfelt Thank you to Developmental Editor, Cathleen O'Connor (www.cathleenoconnor.com) who arranged the chapters and organization of the book and did the final line edits. It was terrific and easy working with you. You did a wonderful job.

Introduction

The journey I take with those who sit with me
is one of healing ...

When clients sit with me for messages, the messages are always about how they can heal and move forward. The strength or depth of the message I receive depends upon the level of pain my clients may be experiencing.

In this world of mediums and psychics, people experience different styles and, most important, different levels of connection. There are the true mediums with depth and clarity that is the gift from God; and there are those who are imposters or have limited capabilities to help others in a genuine and spiritual manner.

My visits with mediums were different from what I experienced when getting messages. As a matter of fact, I felt it was so different I thought I was doing something wrong and that I probably should not be doing this. I was confused because the messages I was receiving were so strong and in-depth, much more in-depth than I received from mediums. I realized this, in fact, is my gift. Mediums will get many souls who have passed, with messages about who they were and about things you did with them while they were here with you. They will tell you about where you are in life but just the surface. The caul will only get a few souls, one of the major differences, as well as what you did with them. The souls will open up the window on your life, where you are now and help you walk through it and get to the other side. They bring greater messages about how you can find your way through what has been holding you back.

The best way to explain how this works for me is that those who have passed on open a door for me to walk through. I like to refer to it as opening the skylight. Another difference is I rarely have more than one to five souls come through where other mediums have many. The messages are also very different. They are deeper and often a message on how my client can heal and move on with their life. This is the gift I have been blessed with as a Caulbearer.

To me, referrals are the ultimate reward and acknowledgment that I'm doing something right. I get or hear "messages" during a session, not "readings", a term I never understood as I am not reading anything. To me, there is a definite difference. The souls, as I like to reference them, bring me the messages. I do not like to use the term spirit or spirit guide as I feel it is not descriptive of those who have passed.

I tell everyone who books me to please not tell me anything. I don't ask any personal questions. I never ask last names just where you are from and if you want to book. I don't have time to go to Facebook or to Google you and I don't have a staff who will do that for me.

I can only give you the messages the Souls want you to have. I have found they always give you what you need to hear at the time you are getting the messages.

If you push for what you want to hear, the way you want to hear it, it will not work. Don't reject the message because it's not the "way" you wanted to hear it. For example, I might see your mate is drinking and has fallen back into his/her old habits. The message I receive is that he/she is not coming back to you and you don't need him/her in your life so move on.

If you are not ready to hear that message you might reject it. But if you want to hear he/she is coming back and I don't see that, I simply can't and will not say it. It's imperative that I am honest, or my gifts granted by God will be taken away. Yes, those of us who are real have received these gifts from God.

There are no books or classes that can teach you this. It must come from above.

This is not an easy path I walk. If you don't have the strength needed to see children who have passed or a mother who is passed and while alive was the daughter's best friend, you can't do this work. It weighs heavy on you in too many ways to address here.

I have been trying to write this book for a few years now, ever since my awakening to all this. Don't get me wrong. I have always been aware that I was born with a veil. I have had unexplained things going on in my life since I was an infant. I heard voices, I knew things that were happening, which affected me and people I knew. The fear of this is what kept me as I like to say, "hiding in the closet."

I received a call from a woman in North Carolina. She had heard that I was born with the veil. Her daughter was also born with a veil and she wanted to know what to expect. I told her I was pretty normal (my family and friends may disagree!) and that I didn't understand much about the whole thing. So, I started looking into this major event in my life to find out more. Most of what I found on the Internet was not right. It just didn't fit until I found Deirdre. She wrote a book called *Born with a Veil* http://www.bornwithaveil.com. Speaking with her opened the curtains on the window of my life for me and I understood why my messages were those of healing and not like most medium readings.

I consider myself blessed and I am humbled by those who are brought to me...yes brought to me, by those in their life who have passed. I pray my gifts continue to get stronger and greater should God choose to allow me to continue on this path. I now understand that it is a path I have had for my whole life. I am convinced these gifts are granted to me by God. Those who are chosen are here to serve others and not make it about themselves. If we get lost on the journey and make this about ourselves or about money, the gift will be taken away.

I had a real problem writing this book because I felt it may seem I am full of myself. I know I open myself to criticism, but this is who I am and what I do, so why bother hiding it. One last thing before I give you the information about the veil: I am told by real Caulbearers (yes, there are those who say it but never lived it and they were never born with a veil) to never seek revenge. Yes, that is good for all, but for us, justice is served up to those who do injustice to the caul...LOL...you know, I have seen that to be true but I never understood it until now.

I have written the book as a series of vignettes and have included the stories of many real-life sittings to illustrate how messages come through me but also because in each person's story I know that you, the reader, will find understanding, connection, empathy and healing as well.

Chapter One
My Story

I came into this world at 4:53am on August 9th many years ago; most likely not as a screaming baby, but rather as a silent one. I was born with a veil on my face. This is known as "The Caul." I am a Caulbearer. There is a lot of speculation and myth surrounding the caul, but I can tell you that my whole life has been a journey with occurrences and happenings that make no sense and are downright confusing to me.

My journey began at about 13 months of age. My mother put me in for my nap at 11:00am with a bottle filled with milk. I heard a voice telling me not to drink the bottle because the milk was bad. I tasted it and it was sour, so I threw it out of the crib. After that happened, I never drank from a bottle again. I remember this as clearly as if it were yesterday.

Years later I would tell my mother the story with precise details. I told her that it was 11:00am and that it was a sunny day when this all happened. At the time my bedroom was a small room off the kitchen. My crib was against the kitchen wall, the window was at the foot of my crib and the blinds were open. My mother confirmed all this including the fact I never took a bottle again.

To this day I wonder who was that very soft voice that I heard.

I have found that when a soft voice comes to me today, the person I'm with is planning to take their life. When I heard this soft voice as an infant I believe that it was God as well because I know that He protects the Caulbearers. I am not sanctimonious, but I have learned to have a strong belief in the Divine Spirits.

This is how I grew up. What you will read in this book are a few of the things that happened to me during my life. Everything you are about to read is true. This is my life and how I dealt with this gift.

I always know when something is about to happen. However, I don't see death, so I never see when someone is about to cross over. I feel this is the Divine Spirits protecting me and for this I am grateful.

Here is one of the visions that I had when I was about eight years old.

On a cold winters day, I went out to the circle at our apartment development to meet my friends Frankie and Jon. During the night the snow had fallen so much that it was very high and up to our chests. Kids in the circle very often played together and we always had a great time. My friends and I were building an igloo, which turned out to be a fort. I was having visions of the computers of today. Computers may have been in the plans, but we knew nothing of them at the time and they wouldn't have looked like the ones we have today. Now visions such as these were not uncommon for me to have, but not understanding them, I just figured I was daydreaming which is how these visions come to me.

Uncle Billy Montauk

It is said Caulbearers do not drown. When I was nine or ten I went on a trip to Montauk with my Uncle Billy. I spent the time body surfing, swimming, and even fishing.

The second day there, I went swimming alone, which as we know, is not a safe thing to do. My Uncle was still sleeping so I got up and went off to the ocean on my own. Suddenly the riptide grabbed hold of me and pulled me down. I was under water for what seemed like an eternity but was more likely just a few minutes. I was about to surrender to drowning because I couldn't fight it any longer and I was losing my strength. Suddenly, a hand came down and pulled me up and out of the water.

It was the hand of my Uncle Billy. He came just in the nick of time and saved me from drowning.

Now I should have been shaken to the core but somehow, I was calm, even though I was giving up or, so it seemed. I was never worried during my time under the water. I always knew I would be okay. It was the strangest feeling I had ever had up to that date.

The Day My Dad Died

At age of 16 on December 20th, my dad went to the hospital to recover from alcoholism, a demon he lived with all his life. My dad was a great guy, funny. There wasn't anyone in my circle of life who didn't like him. He only spanked me once when I locked my mother out of our apartment and refused to let her back in. He was a conductor on the railroad and he had to come back up from Grand Central to White Plains to deal with me. It was a long trip and he wasn't happy; and he had to go back again afterwards to do his run. I get it now.

Dad was trying to kick the drinking when he started seeing things after a few days of not drinking. They thought it was the DTs and took him to the hospital to help him get through it. That same day while in school I was edgy, knowing something was going on and I began to worry. When I got home and didn't see him there my stomach dropped. I was confused and very sad, a deep sadness I didn't understand hit me. They told me he would only be in the hospital a few days and I settled down a bit but was still edgy for several more days.

On December 23rd, at 8:00am I woke knowing my dad was no longer with us. I had butterflies and I couldn't breathe I was so upset. At 8:30am the phone rang. It was the hospital.

I answered; my mom and sister were sleeping still. The voice on the other end requested to speak with mom. I refused to let him and demanded to know what he wanted; yet I knew exactly what he wanted. He insisted he speak with my mom who was suffering from MS that was not diagnosed at the time. I handed her the phone and, as she was getting the news, I felt like I was going to throw up. She completely lost it and she told us dad had gone home.

Later that day when the mail came, I ran to the mailbox knowing my driver's license was there and it was. I had passed. It was the second time I took the test. I needed my License that day to make arrangements for dad. I know now the souls delivered it as it came a few days earlier than expected.

This was the beginning of my never wanting to get these thoughts again, but I was given the strength to get through it and be tough enough to make the arrangements that needed to be made to take care of dad.

I didn't allow myself to cry the entire time of his wake and funeral, keeping strong for Mom, Donna (my sister) and the family. I don't know where that strength came from but the day we buried him, that evening at my Aunt Helen and Uncle John's where the family gathered, I got a message. The message was that "it's okay. You have done what you needed to do." I went into my cousin Johnny's bedroom and silently cried my eyes out.

From that day on I did my best to shut down the voices and the visions. Although I did a good job at it I wasn't always successful.

The Chevelle

Not too long after, I purchased a 1966 Chevelle that I convinced my mom we needed. We did need a car but not that one really. Several of my Aunts attacked me for that.

Me and my buddies were always working on the car, changing the engine, cams, rear ends, etc. I was polishing the car one day when I took a few steps back to see if I missed any polish. Suddenly I had a vision. I saw the front end of the car wrecked in a very specific way. I took a step away from the car, shook my head, rubbed my eyes and looked again but the image I saw was gone. I dismissed it as my being tired. Several months later while driving on a very cold night I hit ice caused by cement trucks that were parked and had been washed earlier in the day. The water from the wash ran across Virginia road and froze causing a slippery hazardous condition.

I lost control skidded to the left and went up on the guardrail. Suddenly, I felt something grab me, pulling me hard to the right. My head hit the rearview mirror and I ended up in the passenger seat. The guardrail struck the steering box which drove the steering wheel into the car breaking the back of the seat I was sitting in. If I had still been in the driver's seat, I would have been killed.

I should mention here that, to the left of the car, was a 10-foot drop. To this day I don't know how my car didn't roll over. There is no doubt that someone pulled me to the right side. It must have been my dad. Hell, I'm sure it was.

Nancy

As a teenager, my girlfriend Nancy and I were very connected. I was just seventeen at the time. I always seemed to know what she was thinking when she was thinking it. One day while walking down Main Street in White Plains, we walked by a candy store and I suddenly said to her, "I'm not buying you that white chocolate." She looked at me and asked how I knew she wanted the white chocolate? I had no answer for her. At the time I passed it off to ESP, which was the common explanation in those days.

This happened to me throughout the four years of our relationship. At the age of twenty, Nancy went to Atlantic City with her girlfriend. I woke at 2:00am sitting straight up. I had butterflies and felt as though I was going to throw up. I became very nervous as I knew she was up to something. There was something happening, and someone was attempting to warn me what to expect. I was told Nancy had met and was with someone else.

When she came home she was very aloof and distant and I knew she was no longer in love with me. I wondered if she ever was. I was also becoming wary of our relationship. After all, we had been together from a very early age.

I asked her what was going on, but she refused to talk and insisted everything was fine; but I knew instinctively and intuitively that was not true.

After several days of this very nervous energy, she finally admitted she had fallen in love with one of the Carney operators on the boardwalk. They met at 2:00am and went for a walk on the beach where they fell in love at the exact time I was shaken awake out of that deep sleep.

Chapter Two
My Awakening

Most of the messages I've received throughout my life were and are just voices warning me of things to come. One of those messages came during a time around 1989 - 1990. At that time the Japanese stock market was flying reaching new highs. They were also purchasing many major buildings here in the US including Rockefeller Center. Many here were concerned they would be taking over the US real estate market.

In June, I was driving with my wife and her friend to the small town of Cold Spring NY, known for its antiques. I was photographing old toys for my book, *My Old Toy Box, Imagination Not Included*. I was thinking about the toys I wanted to look for to include in my book. My wife and her friend were talking about jewelry. Suddenly, I saw the Japanese economy crashing. I loudly said without thought that the Japanese economy is going to crash. The woman in the back seat asked me, "Where did that come from?" I said, "I don't know, but it's going to crash in October." I don't know how I got that. It just came out of my mouth.

It was in October of that same year when the Japanese economic bubble burst. These voices are more like simple momentary thoughts with no rhyme or reason. When that happens, they are always right, and I never know when they will come or why. It just seems to be part of my world that I often don't understand. I am just now learning to accept them without knowing why this happens.

My awakening to all this came when Wayne Gabari, a transformational healer who healed my diverticulitis, preventing me from needing surgery, contacted medium Sheri Perbeck from North Carolina.

I brought Wayne to do a healing on a 4-year-old who had terminal rare brain cancer. I sat in the dining room of the boy's house while Wayne and the boy's parents were in the boy's bedroom doing the healing. While sitting there waiting I had a vision of Jesus. Then a thought passed through my mind that the boy's father was thinking about business while in the room. I thought perhaps I was losing my mind.

When Wayne and the parents returned, Wayne advised the parents he asked several divine spirits to come in to help him heal their son, including Jesus. I thought well he was here. Then the father said, "I'm sorry I wasn't engaged in the room, but I was thinking about a business meeting I have coming up on Monday." I almost fell off my chair and had no idea where this was all coming from. I simply accepted it as a part of my life I had always lived with and didn't give it much more thought.

On the way home from the healing, Wayne placed a phone call on speaker to Sheri. He wanted to see what she saw regarding the healing. She told him she saw several divine spirits around him during the healing. I was driving so I was half paying attention when suddenly Sheri asked who I was. She knew I was there, but she was given messages about me from what she said were seven divine spirits. They told her I needed to do this work.

At the time I had a lucrative photography contract with Con Edison and told her it wasn't happening. We had a bit of a disagreement, but she advised me of the divine spirits and told me I had no choice. She told me to read her when I had a chance and call her back when I was ready. I told her I couldn't do this. She insisted I could and to give it a try.

About two weeks later, while driving to meet with Wayne and his partner Kathy Raymond I started to get visions of Sheri who I had never met. I saw her with black then blond hair. I asked Wayne and Kathy about the color of her hair. They told me black and showed me a photo. With this vision, I saw two men and a woman. I felt the time was right to call her. I explained to Sheri I had always heard voices but never had visions with them. She asked me what I was seeing. I described the first man and told her I felt it was her father; it was. I described the second man. I told her he died in an accident, but it wasn't an accident. I told her two women threw him out of their lives and it was the last straw. That turned out to be her brother who had a fight with his daughter and his girlfriend. As I remember, he has issues he just couldn't get past. The woman was a big woman we couldn't identify. Sheri told me this woman always comes through and that she calls her Bertha.

My next question was about her hair. I told her about the two colors, but I knew she had black hair. She advised me she had just streaked it. It was this reading, and Sheri's belief in me and her energy, that brought me out to this place I am at now. She is responsible for me being here and doing sessions to help others heal.

It was because of Sheri that I gained understanding of how my gift worked and developed confidence in the messages and visions I received. My gift is not only about helping others heal. Two other examples from my family illustrate how my gift helped me and some of my family members heal as well.

Blue Spruce

On December Twenty-Third of 2015, I was heading out to get the family Christmas tree, planning to purchase the usual Douglas fir. As I approached the farm, my dad's soul came to me telling me to get a blue spruce. He was hammering it home. I knew he loved the blue spruce as he had planted one in front of my grandmother's house when he was a young man. Other than that, I had no idea why the blue spruce or what it may have meant to him.

Dad never came to me before about this and I didn't give it much thought at this point. I was even a bit confused why this was so important to him and why he was making such a point of this now.

Finally, after several minutes of this in and out conversation, I asked him what's up with the blue spruce this year. Buying a blue spruce is something that never entered my mind for a family Christmas tree.

He tells me, *"It's my anniversary year, celebrate it by getting the blue spruce."* Anniversary??? I had no idea what this meant; what anniversary it was, or what the reason for this conversation could be. I started questioning what it could be about and began with thinking about the definition of an anniversary. I began putting it together; an anniversary is a celebration of years!

Once I pulled into the parking lot of the farm, I begin counting the years, and that's when I realized today was fifty years to the day dad passed. Wow. It all made sense. Why didn't he tell me this? He wanted me to figure it out on my own, as was his way.

Dad had been very active that year. While driving on Veteran's Day he came to me to ask me to post photos him and his B17 crew which I did. I was asked to start a book on him and our relationship when I was a boy during his time here. He wants me to include his time flying missions during WWII.

I couldn't figure out why he was so active. He is with me from time to time, mostly when I need strength but now he is stronger than ever.

Once I figured out why he wanted me to purchase the tree, I got out of the car and approached the area where the trees were kept. I didn't see any blue spruces. I inquired about finding a blue spruce and its availability. I was advised they don't cut down blue spruces because they are too coarse and hard to handle. Disappointed, I purchased the usual Douglas fir.

I was walking back to the car when right in front of me were several live blue spruce trees that I had passed on the way to look at the cut trees. I had never noticed them. How could I have passed them without noticing them? I was so focused on purchasing what I thought dad wanted me to buy I just didn't notice. No, he had other plans for a tree. He wanted one of the live trees. That tree now sits in my front yard to celebrate his anniversary.

The souls always tell me not to mourn them, but to celebrate their life here with us. This was my validation just how true that is.

For the first time in years, I have the Christmas spirit back...as does my sister. Coincidence? No. There are no coincidences. I know there is a reason for everything. When my dad passed our life became difficult. I am not angry about his leaving us the way he did, or in the shape we were in. No, I wouldn't allow that, and he wouldn't have wanted that for me. What it did was it made me the man I am today, for which I am grateful. I have always found the strength to get through everything no matter how difficult it may be. I have never given up, always keeping the pilot light of positivity lit.

Merry Christmas Dad. I love you. I know you are with me. Thank you.

Uncle Billy Family Reunion

I went to our family reunion recently. Now at parties or events I shut down and try to prevent the souls from coming through, so I can enjoy myself. I also didn't let it be known what I do because I have some who have very strong negative beliefs about what I do. From what I heard, one person there told his wife not to talk to me. We talked anyway, just not about my work.

Well, our Uncle Billy came through. The other family members from that generation were there also, just not as strong or bold as Billy. He was like that when he was here too; but I was wondering why so strong right then. He wasn't particularly my favorite uncle so that wasn't it.

Why did he show up so strong when we were all doing a trivia game? Well, although the trivia questions included all the original family and us, Billy received, by a long shot, the most attention. It wasn't until several moments after the game, as I was questioning him that he pointed out to me he got the most attention.

The one who wrote what I believe to be most of those questions was only his niece, not a granddaughter or daughter. Why did she come up with so many about him and the rest of us took it from there?

I know Billy picked her and it was because she is a very kind, caring and giving person.

At the end of the trivia game, I looked over the crowd of relatives when everything went out of focus for a moment. The only person who was in focus was his granddaughter. I wanted to talk to her, but things got crazy and we just didn't meet up that day.

I sent her an inbox message on Facebook. I told her that her grandfather had come to me along with her husband and wanted to talk to her. We set a date to meet to do a session. The messages she received were how she should move forward with resolving personnel matters which I will not reveal here.

It's funny how the souls reach out to me, getting my attention in some way. Uncle Billy did just that, so he could talk to his Granddaughter; and she received the healing messages she most needed at that time.

Chapter Three
On The Job

One of my life's callings was to become a police officer. It was something I always wanted. I lived and breathed being a police officer.

When I was old enough at twenty-one I took the police test and passed. I applied to Mount Pleasant first because I knew a lot of the officers there, but the chief at the time wouldn't hire me. I didn't push it because it was a slow job and I had this drive to be busy and involved.

I applied also to Greenburgh, NY police department. I was hired and looked forward to the day of becoming a police officer. I was counting the days to my start date. Then one day while working at my Taxidermy Studio I got a call from Captain Crusetto. He informed me they were not hiring me. It seems the vice principal at my high school, Mr. Stone, told them I was insubordinate. I was stunned. How did something I did as a crazy kid several years before keep me from getting the job I always dreamed of?

The next day while working at the Mobil Station, an African American woman came in. She started up a conversation with me. I was so depressed over not getting the job that the last thing I wanted to do is talk to anyone. Even though I had an underlying feeling I would actually get hired, I didn't understand the feeling and simply dismissed it as wishful thinking. She pushed me and we got onto the subject of my not becoming a police officer and why. I don't know who she was or what she did for a living but she told me it's illegal to keep me off the job because of my youthful indiscretions. She told me to call them up, tell them I would take action if they don't reverse the decision, which I did. They reversed their position and hired me.

I have no idea who she was, but she came to me at a very low point of my life, struck up a conversation with me that was meaningful and changed the course of my life. I believe she was sent to me. I cannot prove it, but I can't come up with another reason how she showed up at a very low point in my life to lift me out of the darkness I was in.

I don't believe in coincidences. I believe things happen for a reason. I get the feeling dad may have driven her to me.

Fired Again

About four months into being a Police officer, my lifelong dream finally realized, I was working a telephone company strike. Being on my feet most of the day my right knee began to act up a bit. One of my bosses noticed this and approached me to ask why I was limping. Being a rookie, I was only twenty-one and two months away from coming off probation. I explained to him it was an old football injury but nothing to be concerned about and that it rarely bothered me.

Well, he reported me to the chief. I was about to learn that to be honest doesn't always pay. I was called into the captain's office and informed I was being let go. I couldn't believe this; how could it be happening? The problem was we had unlimited sick leave. What I didn't know was we had one cop taking advantage of the unlimited sick leave. He came to work injured. He faked a fall in the yard and claimed it was job-related. After this fake injury and not showing up to work for years, except to collect his paycheck, they didn't want to take the chance on me doing the same.

I explained to the captain I wasn't that guy. I explained my dream of being a cop and that, at twenty-one, I had every intention of being a viable part of the force. Although my release from the job was imminent, I had that same feeling I've had in the past many times. I knew they weren't going to let me go. Even though everything pointed to me being wrong, I didn't give up. I continued to push, and they decided to keep me, extending my probation for another eleven months. The stipulation was if the injury showed up again I was out. I agreed knowing I would be okay.

Several months later with five more months left on my probation, at 1:00am, we received a call of someone in a house. It had snowed earlier that day and it was slippery out.

As we arrived two people ran from the house, a man and a woman. We gave chase. Just as I caught up with the male and grabbed him I went down twisting my right knee. I ended up in the hospital with a job injury with a witness to what happened.

Now here's why I believe I was being watched over. Because I was still on probation they could have let me go with no explanation as to what their issue was. They could just let me go without any reason. As fate would have it, the couple we arrested that night for burglary were the chief's daughter and her boyfriend, both junkies; and our chief did everything he could to protect them and keep them out of jail. Because of this, the entire issue with my knee went away and the threats of me being released stopped. I made it off my probation with no other issues.

We Are Protected

As mentioned prior in this book I believe that Caulbearers are protected to fulfill their mission while here on earth; to complete a journey mapped out for them. I spoke about not drowning and how my Uncle Billy grabbed me from the grip of the ocean at the last minute. This was not the only time I was miraculously protected.

As a police officer, I was stabbed at, shot at a few times and even wrestled a knife away from a woman with AIDS who was attempting to commit suicide.

Proof positive (as I like to say) of this is another incident. One very cold winter's night while on patrol, my partner and I were driving in a very bad section of our post when I noticed a crowd outside a bar.

I told my partner who was driving and missed it, to turn around. I informed him there was something going on. There was a crowd outside the bar watching a man and a woman arguing. As we pulled over and got out of the car, we were approached by the male telling us the woman was threatening him with a gun. At that moment as we began to approach the angry woman, she pointed the gun right at us and fired three times missing us completely. We didn't have time to draw our guns and return fire before a crowd circled around her, grabbed the gun and the gun disappeared.

She was less than ten feet away from me, my partner and her male friend. At that time we did not wear bulletproof vests. How she missed us is beyond me, but I have a pretty good idea. It had to be divine intervention as there is just no way she didn't hit me or any of us. I was the closest to her and she shot at me first.

The detectives were later able to locate the gun and charge her with attempted murder. The reason for her actions were that she was upset her buddy, who she shot at with us, loaned his girlfriend a blouse of hers. I guess that was as good a reason as any to shoot at police officers.

Again, I was blessed to have avoided serious injury or death.

A Few Other Voices I Heard

While on duty on a foot post I stopped by my regular coffee shop for breakfast. I had been on the job for a while and shouldn't have been on a foot post but that was the way my bosses ran the job. There was a young pretty woman working there. It was the first time I had seen her.

There were those voices again telling me she was the one I would marry. I knew I would marry Janice, my wife, even though there were rough times and forces against us. I always knew we were to be together. Things always just fell into place for us without me even trying. It just happened.

The one final voice I will leave you with was the one that told me my contract with Con Edison as a forensic photographer would end. As much as I tried to prevent it, it did.

The reason it ended was I was making a lot of money. The seven divine spirits I was told about by Sheri were determined to pull me out into this world in which I now live. Sheri and I had an argument regarding my speaking to the other side. I had no intention of doing this, but because they knew I would never do this as long as I was making money doing the photography, they ended the twenty-two-year contract with Con Edison.

It was to be my destiny to do this and, so it is, I am now fulfilling my destiny and my life as a Caulbearer. My purpose is to be there to assist others during their time of need. I realize now that, throughout my whole life, I was always trying to help others; often at my own peril.

This was something I never understood. I couldn't grasp why things happened to me; why I went out of my way to help others I didn't know; why I was to complete my calling as a police officer earlier than I intended.

Whatever it was, I hid from it because I couldn't grasp the difference between the voices I needed to hear and the worry voices which sounded the same to me; and that caused me undue anxiety and worry.

It was the phone meeting with Sheri Perbeck I speak about elsewhere in this book that helped me understand what I needed to hear and why. She taught me to understand which voices I needed to hear and how to listen and interpret them to bring messages of healing to their loved ones here.

So here I am on this journey I was working toward my whole life, one that is not fun, not about me, and not the greatest thing ever. No this is a journey to be there to assist others. This journey often brings pain, anxiety, and a multitude of other emotions.

You may be asking yourself what I get from this. With all the pain it causes me I am gifted with the greatest gift of all: the joy I find and feel when I have assisted others on their way toward living a better life and the life they need to live.

I can simply guide them there, to assist them to walk the path of the new life and find some peace from a life of pain, sorrow, and worry. That is the greatest reward anyone can receive in this life.

Chapter Four
Animal Signs

The Souls will often use wildlife to get our attention. They don't become the animal or bird, but they guide them to us to get our attention.

These are known as signs. Not everything is a sign. The wildlife must be acting very different or unusual to be considered a sign.

A Hummingbird Came To Me

Robin's Mom sent her a hummingbird; I was in the process of a phone session with my client Robin from California. I was sitting on my deck, my dog lying on my lap. I have a hummingbird feeder on my deck but when my dog is there the birds avoid the feeder because the dog tries to catch them.

As Robin's mom is talking to me, a female hummingbird lands on the feeder takes one sip then flies to within three feet of me and hovers there. My dog looks up at the hummingbird and then lays his head back down. I was astonished to see my dog didn't even react and try to catch the bird which he normally would. The mother's voice goes from my head to the hummingbird, but the movie continues to play in my head. She continues with the message from a very different perspective. I was stunned, and I tried to explain what was happening to Robin, but had difficulty finding the words. Her mom tells me she loved hummingbirds. Robin confirmed this. Upon completion of her messages, her mom shows me a hummingbird figurine in Robin's house along with a framed photograph of herself wearing a flowered dress. Robin's mom told me, "that it is where she is now." Robin couldn't understand the message right then and wasn't sure about it.

Later that afternoon I got a message from Robin with a few photos attached. One of the photos was the one I saw of her mother, as well as the couch and the wood-framed opening to her kitchen that I described in Robin's apartment. However, the most important photo Robin sent was a china figurine of a hummingbird her mother had given her. The hummingbird was her favorite bird for sure.

Once the bird was finished talking she began to fly away but stopped, turned around and suddenly my grandmother was there talking to me for a moment. Then the bird turned and flew off. FYI, my dog went back to chasing the hummingbirds once the session was over.

I get some incredible signs from time to time, but this was an amazing one.

The Cardinal Flew To Us

A cardinal showed up to sing as I was doing a session with Denise. Upon my arrival to do a session, Denise and I sat outside on her deck. As her father, who passed two weeks prior, started to come in we heard a cardinal singing off in the distance. As her father's soul got stronger the cardinal came closer and his song got stronger as the messages were coming through until the cardinal was sitting on a tree right behind us, less than 10 feet away. He stayed with us singing on a limb in the tree right above us. His song was loud and beautiful. This continued the whole time her father was giving us his message for Denise.

Once other souls started to come in our cardinal friend began to soften his beautiful songs, a clear sign it was Denise's father who brought him to us.

The cardinal stayed until all the messages were finished before he finally flew off. This was another first for me.

Bluebirds Flocked To Me A Sign

The souls guide wildlife, birds often, to you. My road is a rural road, mostly woods with a few homes. This is not a habitat in which bluebirds live. I have been working with bluebirds at the Rockefeller State Park as a volunteer for many years. I survey the nest boxes keeping track of the eggs, chicks and fledglings. When opening the nest, the parent bird will take off to a tree far off in the distance. I tell you this first because I am about to tell you what happened one Sunday morning when I was in a bad way.

I was walking my dog, Chunk, up the road when I noticed a bird sitting a few feet off the road. Birds that close and that size, are usually a chickadee or a tufted titmouse. They are brave little guys and will stay close to you. But as I looked harder, I saw it was a bluebird. I was surprised, no, shocked! I have lived here for a very long time and have never seen a bluebird in this area; it's simply not their habitat. As I moved closer to get a better look, fully expecting this bird to keep its distance, a dozen or more bluebirds came flying, landing 10 feet or less from me. They were just sitting there. I quickly reached for my cell phone to grab a photo. As I fumbled with the phone about to take the shot, Chunk pulled me. Many of the birds took off flying as I hit the shutter. Fortunately, I was able to get a few in the shot.

I felt some pressure in my chest as this was taking place and I knew it was a sign. But with ego involved, I just couldn't get a clear message as to the meaning. I texted a friend, medium Sheri Perbeck (one of the few I trust) from North Carolina, to ask her. She came back with death. It scared the hell out of me.

I asked if it was me who will die, as I don't see when death is coming. She simply wrote back, nope.

I decided to check out the totem on the bluebird to understand the symbolism. In part, this is what I found. If a Bluebird comes into your life, look for opportunities to touch the joyful and intrinsically native aspects of yourself that you may have lost touch with. Much of what I read was very fitting for me at that point in my life.

I know now it was the souls who surround me that sent the bluebirds to let me know they are there for me. I found this very comforting.

It turned out that the death Sheri saw was that a part of my life changed; a death in a sense of the old giving way to the new.

Gloria and the Dragonfly

My granddaughter, Natalya, was at the house. She was sitting outside playing with her grandmother, Janice, (Lola). Natalya's four years old. Lola noticed she was talking to someone commenting on our garden. two flowers, and how beautiful it is. She then said, to no one, "not you, not you, just you."

She was sitting on the wall next to a dragonfly weathervane talking away, so Janice asked her who she was talking to. She said, "Gloria." Janice asked her how old Gloria was and Natalya replied "80." "What does she look like," Janice asked. "She has brown hair." Janice asked what Gloria was doing. "She is counting money," Natalya said. My son Jarred asked Natalya about Gloria and she told them that Gloria likes being outside because all her friends are at work, and she hasn't been out in 100 years. She is off work and her friends are working.

They went to McDonalds and Natalya told Janice that Gloria was sitting in the seat next to her. When they arrived at McDonalds, Natalya asked Janice, "Can we get a soda for Gloria?"

I wasn't there but when I got home and heard about it, I knew who Gloria was. I have seen many orbs around Natalya every time I do a video of her. It has always been clear she is surrounded by caring souls.

I went to the bank. Driving home I was behind a woman who decided to stop at a green light...how thrilled was I! I'm attempting to get my head around that when a dragonfly suddenly showed up in front of my windshield flying side to side, just hovering there. I put that together with the dragonfly weathervane by the wall where Natalya was sitting talking to Gloria and I had my answer.

My mother died just shy of 60. She died her hair black, but it was brown, as seen in her wedding photo. Although it hasn't been 100 years, that was my mom's way of kidding around. What did my mom do for a living? She was a teller at County Trust Bank. There was no doubt it was my mom.

As though we needed more proof, as we were driving Natalya home the song came on as we hit the parkway...*Gloria*, by Laura Branigan, not a song you hear that often.

The next morning mom woke me about 4:00am to tell me she is watching over the baby.

The Fox Was Crying

I was beginning a phone session in my office with Carol (not her real name). She had recently lost her husband John. I was having serious issues with my cell phone and the call kept dropping. I moved to the kitchen where I had the same issues. This was unusual because I never have any problems like that with my phone. I went to sit on my deck to see how the signal was there and it was fine, so I called Carol back.

Several minutes into our session, I began to hear a crying type noise. It was coming from a great distance off in the woods. It sounded as though it may have been a child or someone in the woods in distress. I stopped talking and listened for a moment and I realized it was not a person, so I ignored the sound and continued with our session. However, the sound was getting louder and closer.

Towards the end of the session, Carol told me that John was a hunter. She asked me if I knew of anywhere she could donate or sell his mounted trophies. He wanted them to go to people who would enjoy them. As she was telling me this, the sound was getting so loud that Carol heard it as well.

Finally, the sound was right behind me. I got up and saw it was a red fox just sitting there crying in my backyard. My dog was quietly sitting on the deck with me watching the fox. Normally when an animal comes on the property he barks and goes crazy!

When I explained to Carol what was happening and that it was a red fox making that sound she was astonished! She said, "Oh my God! I just put John's mounted red fox in my car yesterday to sell to someone. Should I get it back?"

At this point, John's Soul told me it was rare for him to see any foxes and that was the one mount he loved. I told Carol that definitely, she should get it back and keep that one. She told me she would call the guy she was selling it to and ask for it back. Once we established this, the fox stopped crying and just sat there for a few moments and then he walked off.

I am certain that John guided that fox to us because, while I have on very rare occasions seen foxes in my backyard, they never make any noise, nor have they come from such a long way off, letting us know that they are coming.

I question signs at times (I like to be one step ahead of the skeptics). However, putting it all together, here are the events that led to my seeing the fox:

- The cell phone losing the signal where it is normally good.
- My dog Chunk calmly sitting there watching the fox.
- The fox crying the whole time as it traveled a great distance.
- The fox sitting in my backyard crying.
- The fox getting up after Carol and I talked about the fox mount and silently walking off. Had the fox continued to cry as it walked off after the messages, I would not have considered it a message.

There can be no doubt that it was a sign, a very strong sign.

*Note: It's much more common for me to see turkeys, deer, the usual rabbits, squirrels, and chipmunks just about every day. I even had a bobcat back there, and coyotes on occasion. So why did John pick the red fox? I think that is obvious now, isn't it?

I See Horses...

Sam (not his real name) and I sat on the couch. I placed my cell phone next to me. Within a few seconds, after I placed the cell phone down, Pandora came on and a comedian was talking. I was embarrassed and quickly grabbed the phone, shutting it off. I jokingly explained to Sam how these phones had a mind of their own.

Sam is a deep thinker and he was a bit skeptical about our session. His sister often sought out psychic mediums but in his words, he "is on the other side of this." That meant he really didn't believe in this at all. He was, however, open enough to see what it was all about and to see if anything would come of it.

His father and grandmother came in and then his mother, who was the dominant soul of the family. She had just passed the week before and was very talkative--- more so than many souls. The messages were coming in fast. At one point toward the end of our session, she showed me two horses in a corral. I told him about the horses and asked if he or his mother rode horses. It was a strong image. He told me "no, it makes absolutely no sense, at all. There is nothing in our life that would fit that image." However, I knew there had to be something to this because the image was so strong, I advised him of that and we moved on.

Upon leaving his house at the completion of our session, I felt he didn't get what he needed and that there was a lot of misinformation. That never happened before so I was quite surprised. I take this very personally and it bothers me greatly when I feel the person didn't get what they needed. I also know that sometimes people figure these things out within a short time after--often in the next day or so.

Sure enough, Sam contacted me the next day by email and told me everything I gave him, except for the horses, turned out to be right on. He told me he had more questions and asked when we could talk again. We set up a breakfast meeting for the following Saturday.

As I was driving to our breakfast meeting, his mother came to me and told me he had to "man up and stay strong." It didn't make much sense to me as it isn't an issue with him. However, I figured it must be because he was mourning.

Upon sitting down at the restaurant, I placed my cell phone on the table. Within a few seconds, I heard the comedians again on Pandora. I hadn't played Pandora in over a week of seeing him the first time, so it wasn't already open. I quickly grabbed my phone and shut it down, not thinking anything of it.

Once settled down, Sam had a question about his mother's will. He asked me if I saw anything about a ring belonging to his mother. I asked if it was a blue and green ring, which he acknowledged was the ring in question. His mother told me it was meant for his daughter and it was so stated in the will. It turned out it was exactly what his mother wanted, and she did put it in the will.

A few moments after discussing the ring, Sam told me he wanted to show me something. He produced a greeting card his mother had given him. He told me he and his wife were cleaning out closets a few days after our meeting at his house. As they were cleaning out the closets they came across the card he was holding, which he handed to me. The card had a photo on the cover of two horses in a corral. His mother made the card and took the photo and there was a note inside. The first line was about him being a man and staying strong. There it was, pretty much just what his mom had told me in the car on the way over. There were the two horses I had seen in my vivid image the night of our session, which made no sense to him at the time. She was bringing attention to the card which had the meaningful handwritten note to him in it. He had forgotten about it, but she wanted that found.

This was the second time in two weeks where the souls had shown me photographs that were put away and basically forgotten about. The other one occurred during a session with my client Heidi. I saw a photo of a man wearing a white sweater with black stripes on it playing tennis. The man in the photo was Heidi's client, who had passed. Heidi didn't know of the photo or didn't recall seeing it. She advised me she still worked with his wife, and she told me she would ask her about it. When Heidi went to their house, she saw the photo. She sent me a text that contained a picture. It was a photo of her client playing tennis in a white sweater with black stripes on it. His wife found the photo in a drawer and decided to put it up when she rediscovered it.

I never know what the souls from the other side will show me, but I always have faith in them and that what they do show me is true.

As for the phone playing the comedians --- Sam's mom came to me briefly on a Sunday, (the day I shut the "skylight," as I call it, down). It is my day of rest. She told me she liked to laugh and she was the one playing the phone antics. I sent Sam a text about it and he informed me she always told him HE was the funny one! I just wish I had paid more attention to who the comedians were and why this was happening. I know there are no coincidences.

Chapter Five
Dimes

Souls very often show me they are around the person I am in session with. I see lights going on and off, a chair they are sitting in, and they may even show me a vivid picture of a room they are in at my client's house. I rarely see coins for my clients, but they periodically show me coins lying around.

I'd just finished a phone session with a woman in California and she had a question. I had to first tell her that I was seeing dimes that her son whom had passed was leaving around. She was astonished because that was the question she was about to ask.

I began to realize the souls never leave dimes for me. A few weeks after thinking about that, everything started to change. I had just stepped out of the shower and I turned on the hot water in the sink to shave. I had no money on me. I finished shaving and went to turn off the hot water I had just turned on, when I felt something shoved into my hand. I jumped back, opened my hand, and inside my hand was a dime that dropped into the sink. Okay, that may have been a sign. I get that, but I passed it off.

About a week later, I was changing over my pants and I put everything that I had in my pocket on the vanity counter including a lot of change. It was mostly pennies, quarters, and a few dimes and nickels. I pulled the money off the top of the vanity to the front edge with my hand. All the coins fell into my other hand, but I heard one coin drop to the floor. I looked down on the floor to see if I could find it, but I didn't see it, so I just let it go at that point.

About an hour later, my wife came in and told me she found another dime. I dismissed it thinking it must have been the one I heard drop and couldn't find. She then told me it was by the wall between the sink and the toilet. I started to think about how the dime could have gone from the front of the vanity to where she found it. As I was writing this I was shown in a vision there is no way that was possible.

I rethought the events. I scooped the money from the front middle edge of the vanity. I pulled the coins into my hand. If a dime fell 36 inches from the top of the vanity to the floor, it would have had to roll to the left about a foot after hitting the floor, make a 90 degree right turn and roll an additional eighteen inches to where it ended up. As soon as I heard it drop I looked down. I would have seen or heard it roll but I saw and heard nothing other than it dropping.

When I went back later to look at the area again, I realized there is a small area rug on the floor below where I pulled the coins into my hand. Had it dropped from where I scooped the money into my hand, it would have fallen onto that small area rug. I would not have heard it fall and there is no way it could have rolled anywhere.

If you think it is possible for a coin to drop over three feet onto a rug, land on its edge, roll to the left twelve inches and make a right turn, go another eighteen inches before coming to a stop, try it sometime and let me know how that works out! I have to add here, as I'm writing this, my souls are showing me that it is impossible!

A few days later I pulled some paper money out of my pocket and stuck to the bills was a dime, but there was nothing on it to make it stick. All these episodes with dimes are for sure getting my attention.

Finally, I was having breakfast with a friend of mine and I was telling him about what had happened. I pulled the change from my pocket to show him and he looks down and said, "do you see what's on top?" I look down and see three dimes all together right on top of the pile of coins! Yes, someone is sending me a message, but when it comes to my own thing with these scenarios of money, I don't know if I can trust what I'm getting.

The dimes have stopped for now, but the same thing is now happening with nickels! I will somehow figure this all out. The message for you in all this is to take notice of these happenings when they occur to you because the souls are always trying to get your attention. They are trying to let us know they are there. Yes, they are there with us. Just look, listen and hear them. Once you stop missing them and when you are not consumed with sadness, you will start to see the signs.

A Session With Liz

I received a call from a client whose father had died the previous Friday. He suffered from a long illness and was ready to pass. During a previous session I had done for her it came through that her father was tired and ready to pass but he was waiting for an event. The event was a wedding. The wedding occurred and he passed soon after.

She wanted to know if he was happy now, where he was, and another question about what I saw for his passing. She asked if I was free that day and if it was possible to come up to do a session. As things turned out, I had finished my photo assignment early...no coincidence; they never are. She also asked if I could do a session for her husband John and I agreed.

Upon my arrival, we decided to sit outside to do the session. I noticed John was acting as if he didn't believe in this or even want the session, so I didn't push him into doing it. I sat with Liz and her father came through right away. Dad advised me he was brought over by both his wife and mother. He told me he and his wife were and are soul mates. He was in the light and he was finally happy. While he was here, he suffered from a long illness. He is relieved because now he is no longer suffering and has healed and become whole again. During the session, John sat down and listened in. He saw my biggest issue with the session was Liz was extremely enthusiastic and was talking too much, giving more information than I wanted her to give me.

He saw how I continued to stop her from talking. I had to tell her if she continued to talk and give me information about her life with her dad, I would have to stop the session because I wanted the souls to tell me. I advised Liz if she tells me things prior to her father bringing it up, I would not say it because I just don't like to repeat anything someone tells me. It then appears fake. John was impressed by this and with the messages I was getting for Liz. I was quite a way into the session with Liz, when suddenly I turned to him and asked if his mother was deceased. I described the person who was with me and he was amazed at how accurate it was. He confirmed she had passed and it was her.

When his turn came I gave him information from the souls; messages about him and who he was. I stopped for a moment and asked Liz to leave so we could talk privately. The reason was that I saw he was this tough guy with a caring and compassionate man inside. I knew he didn't want that out. I saw him as a savior. I saw the Lone Ranger as his boyhood hero, which he confirmed, and much more. Now he was really listening because he was getting messages I couldn't have known and some of them no one knew. We went on and he went from a non-believer or skeptic to a believer. The session worked for him because he didn't shut it down with his disbelief, as what can and does happen with others.

As we were finishing up, his Aunt came and was with his mother. They are with him, mostly in the kitchen. I asked them to give me a sign. They showed me coins. It happens often with souls. They usually show quarters or dimes. His aunt showed me quarters, nickels, pennies and a lot of dimes. She showed me this because she used to give him coins (mostly dimes) to go and buy candy as a kid which he confirmed.

As we finished I asked him if he was reluctant to do this session. He confirmed he had his doubts until he saw me with his wife and how I wouldn't let her tell me things. He was also impressed how I got things for her that I couldn't have known. Then when his mother came through and I described her, before he could say anything, he lost all doubt. He was amazed at what I saw.

As we were finishing up, his face suddenly changed. I asked him if he was OK. He felt something in his slipper, so he reached down and he pulled out a dime! It was given to him by his grandmother.

Chapter Six
My Healing Purpose

I have been gifted by God to be a Caulbearer. However, I have been confused by this vocation my whole life. As I travel through this road of my life, I don't expect anything in return and I really don't think too much about it, because this is just who I am, and I don't really have the time to spend thinking on it. I have always felt I had a special gift and I was different, but I couldn't figure it all out. A classmate of mine in high school told me she always knew I was different so maybe she was onto something back then. One thing for sure is I am extremely busy doing what I do. I feel there is nothing special here---- hell there are 1,000 mediums around. I'm simply just one of them.

I am a person who has always liked helping people and was the reason I became a cop years ago. I felt being a cop was a calling as is being a Caulbearer. It seemed to be a part of my life where I felt I did what I was truly destined to do.

One evening I was at an event where I saw several people who had been my clients. During a break one of them, Joan, came over to me and said, "Thank you. You saved my life." That simple unexpected statement was so powerful and emotional. I felt like I had been hit in the chest with a cannonball. I was truly stunned. I couldn't understand how I could have possibly saved her life. My sister Donna had originally sent Joan to me. I told Donna what Joan had said. Donna said, "You don't get it. You don't understand how you touch people's lives." Donna is right (but don't anyone tell her I said that)!! However, I still don't get it; after all, I'm only one of 1,000.

Joan's simple, "Thank you" sent a flaming arrow into my subconscious. It sat there slowly burning. I have been trying to put things together ever since. Again, not having the time to spend on it, I just moved forward. Finally, after months of it festering in my brain, I awoke one morning wondering --who am I and what is my purpose here on earth?? I'm just one of 1,000; I have no real purpose here. I am just here to be me and I shouldn't over think it. That day I went to see Brenda, at the request of a newfound Facebook friend. Brenda's son had passed in a fire when their house burned down (see *A Mother's Torment, No More* following). She was led to believe it was her cigarettes that started the fire. I saw an electrical outlet was the cause. That was confirmed by forensics. A firefighter mislead her for his own purposes and she lived with the thought she caused her son's death for nineteen months. It was Brenda's session that changed everything for me. But I still felt I am just one of 1,000.

Many people have come into my life and I must admit that I have traveled some remarkable journeys. As a matter of fact, just the other day, I received a call from a woman in New Jersey. She told me she was looking for the phone number of a woman who was going to help her. She told me, she Googled something in this realm, to find her. 1,000 names came up and all the names were shaded in gray except for mine which was lit up; so, she called to find out who I was. We are now both on a journey. Her parents who she never met came to me. I saw who they were and how they died. She never knew but she had an envelope that followed her as a child throughout her life in foster care. She looked in the envelope the next day. They had died in an accident.

This journey is painful and emotional, but it is also rewarding and healing. I think I may be getting it now. Maybe, just maybe I'm not just 1 of 1,000. I am sure I will struggle with this for some time but perhaps I will find a way to accept this all in the end.

A Mother's Torment, No More

Gianna, a friend on facebook in-boxed me requesting I speak to her friend Brenda who lost her son. I assumed for some reason it was an accident that took him, but I wasn't in my zone so I wasn't sure. Unfortunately, she told me Brenda lost her son which was more than I wanted to know. I prefer to know nothing about the person I'm about to see. I want the messages to come from the souls who come through for my client.

As the session began Brenda's son came through to me, however, before I told her about her son, I told her about others including her parents and her brother, then her son who showed me himself in a blue firefighter's uniform. He was a volunteer fireman. I purposely bring through other souls before the one I know has passed so my client knows this is real. Her son began to show me what had happened. After we went through messages about his brother and sister, he focused on what actually took place that caused his passing; "the color movie", started to play. I saw a house fire. He and another firefighter were in that fire. I saw him with the other firefighter on the other side together.

I saw fire shooting from an outlet and it was unquestionably clear the fire started at the electrical outlet and caused the fire. The house on fire was her house. She had gone food shopping while her son was still asleep in the house. She began to cry as she was telling me she felt that she was the cause of the fire because she threw cigarettes in an ashtray in the garbage (even though she was sure that she had put them out before doing so). I reiterated it was very clear in my "color movie' the fire was caused by a faulty outlet. I then asked her what they found was the cause of the fire, what was the fire department's findings. She told me the fire department deemed the cause as unknown; however, one of the firefighters who battled the fire blamed her for throwing her cigarettes out in the garbage. He blamed her for causing both the deaths of her son and the other firefighter. I told her "No. I saw the garbage on the other side of the room from the outlet." She confirmed that, but still believed she was at fault because one fireman was still blaming her and convincing her that she was the cause.

Then the other firefighter who passed in the fire, came to me patting his chest, telling me it was a heart attack and not the fire that caused his death because he was out of shape. She validated that, but she told me the others were still angry and they felt she was the cause of the fire and both of their deaths. The firefighter soul who came to me, told me this particular firefighter is shady and that I shouldn't believe him.

When we finished with the messages, I asked if she ever found out the real cause of the fire because it was revealed to me through my vision the outlet was the cause as seen in the "solid movie" they played for me. I told her that there had to be a fire investigator who uses science to find the cause. What was his finding? She told me the insurance fire investigator found the fire was caused by a faulty outlet, across the room from the garbage. I told her the movie the souls played for me was what the investigator found and I saw it before her telling me what happened. I asked her why she believed the firefighters. I explained how I saw there was a purpose for them saying that, even though they didn't really know the cause. It turned out one fireman was claiming he hurt his back in the fire and was suing her. His suit would be worth more if the cause was negligence on her part. Later that evening she sent me a text. She told me she found out this fireman, who claimed he was injured in the fire, was shady and he had injured his back prior to the fire. I reminded her the souls told me he is shady and obviously he is.

She realized what her son and the other souls showed me made sense, and she could now believe the fire investigators report. After nineteen months she could finally believe she wasn't the one who killed her son by throwing out the cigarettes, and the shady fireman's accusations were untrue. He was only putting out a false fabrication for his own benefit. This was terribly devastating for a trusting innocent woman, who believed all firefighters are heroes and honest. She now knows this isn't always the case.

My message from this session. When I awoke the morning I was going to see her, I was questioning myself and God as to what my purpose is here on earth. I have nothing to contribute to this world--no great inventions, no big events. I wasn't feeling good about myself. My answer came in this session when I saw the difference the session made in Brenda's life. Brenda could now live her life knowing it wasn't her who caused her son's death, as she had for the last nineteen months. Perhaps it's not about the masses, it's about helping and healing one person at a time. I can't tell you how rewarding it was to see this woman heal and get lifted by the souls out of the depths of darkness. Perhaps I am here to help one person at a time, but it just doesn't seem like enough to me. This question will always be a part of my life. It's who I am.

The Reality of This Gift – Lou Lou's Story

Part of the Caulbearers experience is feeling the pain of those who have passed. Occasionally I can't move on from someone who has come through, after helping that person I'm with to move down the path to healing. This is a burden we bear; I consider this part of the sacrifice I make and suffer, in return, for this gift. I know the souls don't feel pain, anger or hatred and we become whole again once we have crossed over. I now know they can be sad. I recently saw this, but it's not the sadness we suffer from here. This pain is for others who can't move on with their lives due to their passing. Understand I'm not saying stop missing them or don't have some sadness, not at all, but some here become paralyzed from the pain.

Very recently I had an experience that affected me more than any other. It was around a child who passed. I have had many children and it's always very painful, but this child (her name is Sophia) stayed with me. The day after I met with Sophia's mother she sent me a private message thanking me for the messages, letting me know it was helpful. Upon reading that the pain was so strong, my heart was so heavy, and I became very emotional. Although this has happened before, this was far and above the magnitude of all others.

Sophia told me she was sad because her daddy was in a great deal of pain even though he hides it. I wrote her mother and offered to meet with them together. I told her I would not charge for this, because one, this can't be about money all the time and two, I didn't want any suspicion by the dad that I would be coming to make money off their grief. I didn't mention this to her, but I saw a uniform for him. I wasn't sure if he was a police officer or a fireman. I asked if he would be open to this. She asked him and told me that even though he was skeptical, he was open to hearing what I had to say.

Upon my arrival, I found he was a firefighter and in his uniform. I was surprised to realize I knew him. I didn't know him well. He worked at a Fire and Police supply store I went to on occasion where my friend worked. I had no idea he had lost a daughter. As I began our session, I have to admit I was a bit nervous, not for me, but because this was very important for their daughter Sophia who wanted him to not just hear her message but believe it, believe in her. Sophia had been sending them messages, but he wasn't seeing them like his wife has been.

Upon my walking in, the dad was glaring at me like someone who was pissed at me for something awful. However, within moments I was told by one of the adult souls who were with me that he didn't want to become emotional and that made complete sense. I wasn't sure if he got anything from the messages. I rarely am, it's just who I am.

I did speak with his wife later who told me he will need time to figure things out; again something that is normal with this modality. I realized my heart felt lighter when I left after our session. I believe this was because he did get something out of the session. At the very least their daughter got to talk to her daddy and that was all she wanted to do.

I am rarely up at 5:00am but when I am there is a symphony of birds outside my window singing. The morning after our session I was awakened by a single cardinal, at 5:00am sitting and singing outside my window. Cardinals are one of the birds the souls often use as a sign; one that had significance for this family. What actually caught my attention was this was the only bird singing at the time. I've never been awakened at that hour by a single bird, and this bird sat there and sang for a half hour until I realized he was sent to me as thank you from Sophia. There is no doubt in my mind and I have to be convinced when it comes to messages for me. I am not the kind of person who believes everything is a sign.

A few days later I spoke with her mother and told her about the bird. I jokingly said to her how I wished she waited until at least 6:00 or 7:00am. Her mother told me she woke up at 5:00am every morning.

Several days later another cardinal with a very deep voice showed up and sang outside my window, again at 5:00am and alone. The day before that bird showed up I had done a session for a man whose brother came through. This cardinal was sent by his brother who came to me the day before. He too was thanking me for being there for his brother. "Hey, birds pick a later time please!" The next morning it was back to the symphony of many birds.

Sophia being very active with me gave me several signs in the days after her father's session. One morning, after pouring syrup on my waffle, I went to the sink to clean off the top, and there was very little syrup left in the bottle. All of a sudden, I had syrup all over my hand. That has NEVER happened before. I couldn't figure out where the syrup actually came from as there was too little at the bottom to flow over onto my hand. I knew it was Sophia being playful. As I'm going to wash my hands I actually began licking it off my hands. I never do that but for some reason, I was doing it. I stopped and went to wash my hands, when I heard Sophia say, "don't wash it off, it feels and tastes good." It was right then when I heard the voice that I knew this little girl was with me again this morning in a playful way. I realized she was playing a little trick on me; it's the only way this could have happened. Later when speaking with her mother and telling her what happened, she advised me Little Sophia used to put syrup on her hands and played with it licking it off.

NYC Firefighters – 9/11

I had done a session for an NYC Firefighter Carl and his fiancé Barbara. I saw a fatal auto accident. I described it very accurately including the fact that they had been cut off by another motorist. The survivor in the back seat confirmed this in his statement to the police validating what I saw. In my vision, I saw a woman who had passed in the passenger's seat. She came through to me right away. I also saw a young man there who passed as well but didn't seem to want to let me know who he was. My attention kept being drawn to my client's refrigerator in their kitchen. It was about 20 feet away from where I was sitting. There were many photos on it but one, in particular, had lit up to me as I looked at the refrigerator door. I couldn't see who it was from that distance, but it held my attention.

As usual, at the end of the session, I asked if there was anyone who hadn't come through that they wanted to hear from. I felt the shadowy figure was waiting for someone to ask for him. Carl said Jim, and I responded, "he was in the car, he was the driver---it's your son." Carl confirmed it was and that he was waiting for him to come through.

It turned out the photo on the refrigerator was a picture of Carl's son. They went and got the photo to show me without me asking. I didn't tell them about it lighting up. They just went and got it. I wanted to know from the son why he took so long before letting me know who he was. He told me his dad was angry he had passed and he wasn't sure if his dad wanted to hear from him. He also felt if he had come through sooner his dad wasn't really ready to hear from him.

Carl was angry. Jim was going to be his best man at his upcoming wedding. Jim apologized he passed too soon and asked for his father's forgiveness.

We finished our session and we were talking about fishing. Suddenly, I saw five NYFD firefighters' souls walking from the towers across the street to a firehouse. I asked Carl if there was a station across the street from the towers and he confirmed there was. I told Carl about the one firefighter I recognized and described him. He said that's Sean Tallon. Carl knew Sean and Sean was out of the house across the street. I saw a total of five firefighters who walked from the towers to a firehouse across the street. They cleaned up and they sat down to watch TV. One was extremely tall. Seven feet to be exact. My client also knew him. They were friends. He was an NYFD paramedic, but he didn't pass in the towers, he passed later on. These five souls chose this moment to come through and Carl had a connection to two. The others were with them; they stand together and wanted Carl to know they are with him.

When I got home a 9/11 scene was with me. It was awful and something that I had never seen before. I have to be honest here; it was so painful that I broke down when I got home as the five firefighters were still with me.

There was one in particular who stood out. He was short, and he wanted to contact his family. I don't know who he is or if that will ever happen, but he is with me now as I write this. His wife/fiancé is still struggling.

The fire station "house" directly across the street from the towers was "Ladder 10" I was told. I continued to investigate to see if I could find out more about this, but I was never able to find out anything further about the house across the street and my clients never contacted me again, so I was never able to validate much of what was in my vision.

I will make this offer: if anyone who reads this is or knows a first responder's family, someone who is really struggling with the passing of a loved one, I will do a session for them for absolutely no charge.

My Daughter Is Missing

One Tuesday night, I received a call at 9:00pm from my client Ann. She was in distress she told me her 28-year-old daughter Carol had been missing in Florida since Saturday. Carol wasn't responding to calls or texts and her calls were going directly to voicemail. Carol's boyfriend told the mother she left to visit her uncle but never arrived at the uncle's house.

My first instinct and thoughts were logical on this side, the obvious--someone grabbed her. Suddenly, I remembered a story I'd heard about Sylvia Brown, who told a mother her daughter, who was missing for three years, died. This caused the mother to get sick and eventually she died. The daughter was found alive a few years later. Recalling the story from just a few days prior made me withdraw and stop those thoughts, pull back and go deeper to the other side than I have ever gone before. This was a new gift for me.

I asked Carol to come to me and tell me where she was. I got no answer. Carol didn't come to me. I knew at this point she was not on the other side. Then the souls for the mother came to me, telling me she was with a boyfriend or ex-boyfriend. I described the man to Ann as having a scruffy beard, small and thin, including the fact that he rode a motorcycle. Ann told me that was the ex-boyfriend. I told her she was in a two-story complex. Ann told me that is where she lives. I told her this was close to where she lived but not the same one. I advised Ann to call the police and file a missing person's report. The report would help find her daughter.

Wednesday morning, I was seeing the daughter in a pool or water and I was getting messages about her car being parked by the pool. I called Ann to tell her. She advised me she was just about to call me. She called the boyfriend and the ex-boyfriend to see if they heard anything from Carol both said no. She advised them she was calling the police to file a missing person's report just as I had advised her to do. Within five minutes Carol called Ann. It turned out she went to the ex-boyfriend's place to be with him, which was a two-story complex that had a pool. His place was near the daughter's.

This is a great ending Ann told me. Carol was advised if she ever did this again, "there would be more to come from her for doing such a thing." I take that to mean Ann would rain down hell on her. Had it been one of my kids, I would have been on a jet that very moment to have a serious talk face to face.

The important thing here is I stopped my logic on this side, from getting the better of me, as many in this modality often do. I went deep to see what I could get before saying anything to Ann. This is why being real is so important when you do this.

Text Messages For Mom

I receive a text out of the clear blue from Charleston, North Carolina.

"LOEV. HOOAS"

I texted this person back with, "????"

The next thing that happened was my phone started to ring. The call coming in was from a woman asking me if I texted her. I responded, "No, you texted me." She proceeded to tell me she did not send me a text. I asked her if she knew me or if she ever had a session with me. The answer was no.

She was an elderly woman sometimes hard to understand. I explained to her who I was and what I did. She had no idea, so I then asked her if there was someone who cared for her because she seemed to be a little confused. She told me there was. When I asked to speak with that person she never put me on the phone with her.

For days these texts would come in making no sense, to me. She would call me after each one and ask if I sent her a text that made no sense. Each time I would let her know it was coming from her phone.

Finally after about a week of these senseless texts we got: "LOEV. HOOAS. 2000"

I began to connect with the other side as she acknowledged HOOAS meant something to her. I told her I was hearing a man's voice. This man who was only talking to me told me he was her son who passed in 2000. When I asked her about this, she confirmed it. It was then I could explain to her what the message was saying.

His message for her was LOVE HOOAS 2000. He was sending her his love through text.

When they do use the phone and text, the text is mostly unintelligible gibberish with a few words mixed in we can make sense of. Once we established who it was from and what he was trying to say, the texts ended.

Although I asked the woman who or what HOOAS was, she never clearly explained it, however, I was getting that it was her son's nickname.

Ice Cream

When talking with the souls, I get messages they don't totally explain.

I was speaking with my client, Joan whose mother, grandmother, father, and husband John came through to me. After her mother and the others finished saying what they had to say about their life with Joan, both as a little girl and a grown woman, her husband John came forward and gave me what he wanted Joan to hear from him, part of which I will now share.

John had been sick, and he had suffered for a very long time. He told me his daughter was daddy's little girl. Before you say aren't all daughters' daddy's little girl, I have to tell you "No they are not." Very often I hear how they are not close to their dads at all. Just to divert for a moment---such was the case in one session where there were three sisters sitting with me. Their dad told me only the middle daughter was daddy's little girl. I apologized to them when it came out and all three laughed. I didn't tell them anything they didn't already know. The statement was true and they all got a kick out of it. I only get messages about daddy's little girl when it is true, which isn't as often as you may think.

One of the things John brought up early in his message was he wanted Joan to get out of the house more. He told her to go out for "ice cream." I saw the image of a vanilla ice cream cone. John referenced ice cream several times during our session. If you know me, I don't let my clients talk until they know I'm real. When the ice cream cone first came up, I thought it might have been symbolic, but he told me she should grab her daughter and go out to get ice cream with her. At this point, their daughter is not a young child anymore.

John then showed me an image of an old-fashion ice cream parlor. I asked Joan if there was such a place near where she lived in Queens. She told me there was. I told her John wanted her and their daughter to go to that particular place and have ice cream.

As we were finishing up the session I asked Joan about him making so many references to ice cream. I told her I didn't feel it was symbolic and I asked if it was meaningful to her about taking their daughter out for ice cream.

She said, "when our daughter was a child, she asked John to take her out for ice cream." He told her, "no, they would go out another time." That never happened; life seemed to always get in the way, and they just never got around to it. It bothered him until the day of his passing. Joan told me he would reference that often throughout his life and how much it bothered him that he never followed through on his promise when she was a little girl.

As we finished the session, we were talking about the ice cream and how much John wanted the two of them to go out and get ice cream. She told me that she would do it. Suddenly, the vanilla ice cream cone which I had been seeing throughout the session, became a hot fudge sundae! I told her what John said, she got a real kick out of it. We both had a good laugh as we were hanging up the phone.

I do hope they will do it together soon.

Bob Wanted To Know

I was doing private sessions for a party of five. The third person comes in, his name is Bob, and he is in his eighty's.

Bob and I sit down, and the souls come in for him including his daughter who wasn't a nice person while she was here and didn't talk to us much during our session.

Bob received messages about his sons who are still with us and how close they are to him. It came through that Bob was hurting, feeling let down and alone. It was also clear Bob was always there for others when they needed him. The souls showed him how his family is there for him and how much he is appreciated.

At the end, I felt Bob was still in pain, but I was on a time limit of thirty minutes and our time was coming to the end. I asked Bob if he had any questions. He responded how right on I was all the way through, but asked me to ask his daughter a question.

I hate this because sometimes they do not answer questions. I asked him what his question was. He asked me to ask his daughter "if she had anything to say and why she said what she said." That wasn't much to go on, but I told him I would see if she would answer that.

I shut my eyes and went down deep, as I call it. His daughter was sitting on a horse, just looking at me. I asked her what she had to say and she refused to talk. After about five minutes of this, knowing I was going over on the time, I forcefully said to her, "You have to tell me what Bob wants to know and do it now!"

Finally, she said to me, "Tell him I know he loved me and I'm sorry I said that."

I opened my eyes and repeated it to Bob.

He looked at me and started to cry and told me that days prior to her passing she told him, he never loved her and that he only loved her brothers. That wasn't true, but it was extremely hurtful to Bob who carried that with him for five years.

He told me he has been going to mediums for the past five years and no one was able to answer that question. Bob received the message he so desperately needed to hear. He now knows his daughter is sorry for saying that and she never believed it, only saying it to hurt him. That is who she was here.

Bob is at peace with his daughter now, a much needed and deserved peace.

Two Years Later

I had a session with a Bonnie who I gave messages to at a party two years ago. I knew we had met before and I knew

64

where, as well. As usual, I couldn't remember what her messages were. If I remember anything about sessions, it's usually only the highlights.

The messages this time were around her marriage and her business. Her Grandmother came to me first then her two Grandfathers. They showed me Bonnie's struggles and the tug of war she is going through. Bonnie has some serious choices to make. She is very unhappy, and the choices are very difficult. I saw resentment building, growing into anger and then hate. Her grandmother was telling her to respect herself. I am not here to tell anyone what to do; I just deliver the messages. It is up to my client to decide whether to follow them or not; however, the souls can be pretty persuasive.

The session went well. They showed me that Bonnie was not only logical, but she was extremely creative. They didn't give me what she did this time like they had the first time. She remained completely silent as the session went on, which is how I like it and what I prefer. I noticed it was making her a little uptight. She wanted to confirm things, which is Okay, as long as she didn't say too much.

After her messages were complete, I asked her about the first time we met, because I didn't remember. She told me everything I had told her at the time was happening. This isn't the power of suggestion type of thing, like, you're going to purchase a red car on Thursday and you do. But rather, these were life's events that no one has control over. As we spoke about her first session, it came back to me. After I finished her messages during our current session, it was clear that she was not happy. I thought at the time maybe they gave her messages that were wrong, but that has never ever happened.

As we spoke, she told me she didn't like the messages, which is why she left the way she did at the end of the prior session. Bonnie apparently went to other mediums and received "better" readings, which were more to her liking, but mine were the only ones that were right on. As a result, she came back to me, and this time she listened.

My calling as a Caulbearer is to give messages the souls want those who are brought to me to hear. It is not always what they want to hear. I never say what they tell me without further questioning them before saying what they give me. I am somewhat of a skeptic, so I question them a few times about what they tell me before I say it. This is just one more of a long line of lessons I get from the divine spirits. They tell me I must believe in the messages and because I never ask leading questions, there is no way I can guess or make something up.

If I no longer hear the messages of the souls or if the divine spirits decide to take away my gifts, I will walk away from this with honor. I will know that I gave many messages out that clients needed to hear and at the right time when they needed to hear them.

This is not about me. It's about the souls and the divine spirits who have chosen me to speak through me to their loved ones. I don't care about being right for me. I must be right for you. I have simply been chosen and even through all the pain that comes with this, I am forever grateful that I have this gift.

Chapter Seven
Messages

We get messages as we need them, even me...BELIEVE!

I put great importance on the gift that God has granted me. Some say I put too much on what I get and what I give to people. Perhaps this is true, and one day I will accept the fact that I just simply can't help everyone. However, knowing me, this is most likely not going to happen because I want to be there to help whenever I can.

The other night I did a small party consisting of five people. The first two came through and everything went very well. Then the third one Kate comes in and I had three female souls with me for her. However, I was struggling with them and who they were. I saw a woman with long black hair. Kate said she didn't know who it was. Then I got her mother who told me what her daughter had done for her as she was passing. These were very strong messages. However, Kate told me nothing was making sense to her. I just thought she wasn't getting what I was saying through the validation process or she wasn't hearing what she was hoping to hear. (I can only give clients what the souls want them to hear.) So the mother started to bring attention to her father and her boyfriend who are still here. She acknowledges the information was "pretty" correct, except for the height of the boyfriend, so she dismissed the whole thing as not being right. Even though everything else she received about him was correct. It was at that point I ended the session. Her mother and Grandmother (the second woman who came to me) left me. They do that when you make them struggle and when you don't believe in them.

After all the sessions were over, we all came together. I asked Kate if her mother had short blond hair, not platinum, but blond. The mother showed me that earlier but I had stopped saying anything because nothing I said seemed to be right. She said "no", but the woman next to her said, "yes she did." Kate pulled up a photo of her mother on her phone and showed the others. I never saw the picture. Everyone told her it was blond hair. She didn't agree with them. Most were hair dressers so I thought, they should know. As it turned out Kate is a skeptic. As a matter of fact, her mother told me she doesn't believe in anything! That didn't matter to me because I was still down about that session which caused me to question all the sessions I had that night.

Now things happen when you need them to. Never doubt that. The next morning, I woke up to a text from Frankie with whom I had done a lot of work. He didn't need to say this but he tells me all the time about how I am always there for him. I'm guessing the Souls and the Divine Spirits knew I needed something because I was very close to giving this up. Frankie telling me what he did brought me back to where I needed to be.

I am thankful for everyone who comes into my life and this will never change. The following is what shook me awake that morning, in more ways than one.

Gmornin brother. I'm at work in the truck and I just been reflecting on the past year and I really just wanted to say thank you. I know I've thanked u in the past but sincerely truth of the matter is if you weren't around at that down point of my life I prob wouldn't be here today to talk about it. U took me out of a place that was so dark and treacherous I just don't think I could ever repay u for it. Thanks again for being a great friend to me.

Later that week I heard from the sister of the host of the party Kate was at. She told me Katie started to realize that most of what I gave her made sense after all. It took her a few days after the session to realize this. This often happens and it is why I now tell my clients that I will go with whatever the souls give me, not what my client says. This happens all too often.

I Listen To The Souls

When it comes to listening to my client or the souls--- it's the souls I listen to every time. Here are two examples why. Recently I was told by Mary's grandmother that Mary, who I was in session with, needed to change her life in certain ways. She also showed me how close she was with Mary and some of the things they did together. Mary didn't think some of those things happened. Mary was looking for a specific answer in her love life. Honestly, this is something the souls don't seem to like to talk about. I told Mary what I was told by her grandmother, which was she had to do something for herself; fix herself so she was ready for a relationship.

However, Mary dismissed that, and she wasn't sure she should believe what was being said because I wasn't telling her what she hoped to hear. The next morning at 3:00am the grandmother woke me up. She really wants Mary to listen to her. I texted Mary later that morning telling her about the 3:00am wakeup call I had from the other side. Christ, I wish they would wait until at least 7:00am! Coincidently Mary was also awakened at 3:00am thinking about her grandmother. Mary also told me she talked to her mother after our session who validated everything I had told her, including what grandma showed me, which was what her and her grandmother had done together. I also gave Mary a few names in the text that were very meaningful.

By the way, names are not usually my thing. Had I listened to my client she wouldn't have gotten the messages she now knows she has to listen to. The next step on Mary's journey is up to her, but the souls can be very persuasive.

A few days later I was with a Rebecca. I described a short woman by the name of Jane with long dark hair. Rebecca didn't know this woman. Then the movie started to play. I saw this woman who had been stabbed to death and she was dead on a couch. Because Rebecca didn't know her, I didn't get very deep into the whole thing. I told her to look into the building that we were in because the murder I was seeing was an old homicide and may have happened there as the building was an old building. I also told Rebecca to ask her mother about Jane. I learned later from Rebecca that she asked her mother and her mother found out about two weeks earlier that a great aunt by the name of Jane was stabbed to death while she slept on the couch in 1948 in Queens by a mentally ill neighbor who was related to her. Had I stopped and ignored Jane we would have never found out about her and who she was.

When They Tell Me Something

What I have learned over time is that when the souls tell me something, I must go with it. All too often when I am giving a message to someone, they will tell me it doesn't sound right. After a day or two, they begin to recall it is right. This is often called psychic amnesia---wherein they are getting so much information they just don't remember it all.

I have two great examples from when I first started doing this for others. The other day I was doing a private session. I was getting messages for Joan and what was coming through to me was that her deceased ex-husband liked boats and fishing with his son. Joan told me no. I proceeded to tell her I had a very strong image of big boats, a large body of water and him fishing with his son. She told me no, we don't have a son and that doesn't make any sense, so I let it go. Joan called me the next day to tell me she called and spoke to her daughter about our session. She was the one who originally referred Joan to me. Her daughter told her, the ex-husband very often would go to Cape Cod where he loved to go whale watching. It was one of his favorite things to do; hence, the big boat and the water. He also went fishing all the time with his son from another marriage! When I was initially receiving the message from him I let it go because she wasn't connecting with it. Her ex didn't continue on so we never got to find out where he was going with his message.

The second example is about Jessica, brought to me by my client Lorraine, whose husband had passed. Lorraine sat in the session as well as the woman's son Jim. I was getting her late husband worked with his hands. She said no, so I let it go. Then he was showing me he was fishing with Jim. She and Jim both said no; again, I let it go. Well, this man was a part-time actor. A few days later I got an email from Lorraine who was originally sitting in with us at the session, and here is what she wrote:

"I want you to know after you left, her son told his mother, his father did work with his hands. He did maintenance for an apartment, so you were correct. Also, they showed me a DVD of the commercials he did. One was one of him fishing with his son so maybe that is what you saw."

So, you see, when the souls give me something there is a reason. When I get messages, I give my client everything the souls tell me. I have found it will make sense later if it doesn't make sense at the time.

I was wondering why the father would have shown me him fishing with his son Jim. I was told it was a TV commercial, not real life. Lorraine explained to me before I got there to do the session that Jim asked his dad to show him the commercial and then he would believe me. Well, the dad came through for both of us because Jim had just forgotten about what the commercial was all about when he told me him fishing with his dad didn't make sense. His dad was proving to him I was real.

I understand why people like to test us, but it doesn't always work. The souls don't like being tested and they don't give us what the client is asking for at times.

An example of this is when I was doing a phone session with Joe who was not a nice person. He was condescending, obnoxious and just being a jerk in general. Long story short. I nailed a lot for him all of which he confirmed to be 100% correct, but he then said to me "everything you said was 100%

correct. I'll believe you if you can tell me what my wife would say when she got mad." She just wouldn't come through and give that to me that night. However, the next day I woke to hear,"Drop dead and go to hell!" She was giving me this all day. She didn't give it to me the night before because she told me Joe was acting like a jerk and she was right. But I still wish she would have given it to me that night. I never called Joe to tell him what she said came through, but it was confirmed by someone who knew them both.

The souls work in strange ways sometimes.

The Souls Are My Only Search Engine

People come to me seeking answers, I have the reputation of helping people heal through the messages I receive from the other side. As I have said throughout this book, I am forever thankful for the privilege of being granted this gift which allows me to assist others. The souls give me what they want you to have the time of the session. It is information important and pertinent at the time. Once I pass on their message, I give my client a chance to ask questions of the souls.

Then there are the non-believers. I'm fortunate I don't get many of them. Some of them come to me to prove I am wrong or to prove I am a phony. Others come who want to hear from the souls, but they don't believe the message unless they get solid proof. They want to hear from someone specific who always comes through, but often question the messages they are given. This is more prevalent with men. As with all skeptics, I understand this as well as their concerns

I wish I could show them on a screen what I see, but there simply isn't a screen. Although souls understand the skeptics, they expect some faith in them. I find when someone comes to me who refuses to answer questions that have no effect on the messages, it makes it very tough. A question such as, how did you find me? Sometimes they don't even want to give me their first name or phone number (I never ask last names). When this occurs, I ask the souls why. They say it is because someone doesn't have faith, or they are being dishonest.

I never ask leading questions, and when I ask a question it's because something is coming in, and I explain to my client, any question I ask requires they answer yes or no, nothing more.

I recently received a call from someone I'll call a 'Man of Science." He reached out to me wanting a phone session. I asked him how he found me, but he didn't want to tell me. I told him I only wanted to see if he searched the net or if he was referred by someone. He then told me that some people I gave messages to had sent him. He wouldn't tell me who. I told him it didn't really matter as I most likely wouldn't have remembered them anyway.

During the session, I received quite a bit of information from his father and mother, but he seemed skeptical all the way through to the end of the session. The souls showed me his failed marriages. He didn't seem to believe what he was getting but acknowledged it was true. I didn't understand this. Later on, after the session, I saw he was very logical and focused in his work. I asked what he did for a living, but he said I should know without having to ask. However, because he was so difficult, messages came through slow and hard.

Finally, toward the end, he was a bit upset because someone didn't come through. As always, I asked him for a name. He didn't want to say, and he told me that was too much information and she didn't come through because she didn't want to. I started getting his sister and honestly, the woman I was seeing wasn't right for who he wanted so he abruptly ended the session. He didn't give the soul a chance to come completely through. Things come slowly, and the souls often take me 40 miles to get to that mile, but it is always for a good reason. So, we must let things develop at the right time and pace. The next day, I had someone come to me who I believe was one of his ex-wives. I e-mailed him the information, but he never answered, so I don't know for sure if it was her or not.

The point here is if you don't have some faith, the souls will come through but not as strong. At the end, he thanked me for "not Googling him," but not in a nice way. He was a very difficult client all the way through. The fact is I never Google anyone because it is not about me being right, but rather it's about the message.

He paid by PayPal. When I checked the payment his last name was there, so, you guessed it, I had to Google him. All that was there was his profession. He was a dentist. I got nothing else. Nothing about his relationship with his parents, or who they were, or anything else that came through during his session.

This is one of the many misconceptions about mediums which are spread by nonbelievers. People believe we Google them, really??? Just how much of anyone's life is on the net? One thing is for sure, nothing about your childhood or your relationship with the souls and for damn sure nothing about what you're going through on a personal level.

My clients who have been with me know what you get can't be found anywhere on the internet. Hell, I don't have the time and I really don't need to. Why should I? The souls are my search engine and they are the only ones I need and trust.

The Ambush

One day I was sitting in family court. I was in a room with several other people. Now those of you, who either have been with me or follow me, know I never do what I call the ambush. That is when you're in a public place and get something for someone---you would then approach them. It rarely happens with me because I don't feel it is the right thing to do. I control the souls I don't let the souls take over, I never say anything to the individual.

There was a woman sitting talking to her attorney. She looked tough, but I was involved with other things, so I didn't pay too much attention to what was going on. Suddenly I had a woman about 5 feet in height and strongly built with me. She was telling me that she was here for the woman who was with her attorney. She had a lot of food, so I thought it was her grandmother, but then I heard that it was her mom. She wanted me to give the woman sitting there a message. I told her no because I don't do that and that I didn't feel comfortable because her attorney was sitting with her. The next thing I knew her attorney left the room for a minute and I was fighting back and forth with the soul about whether I should do this or not. Then her attorney came back, so I told this soul I would talk to her relative if the attorney left again. I was pretty sure her attorney wouldn't leave but to my surprise she did. I shouldn't have been surprised as this soul was very insistent on me talking to the woman.

I moved over and asked her if her grandmother had passed. She said no, and she asked me if I was a psychic. I explained to her who I was. I told her who was with me. I told her that this woman appears to be tough, but she is actually very sensitive. When I told her what I was getting, she confirmed it. I was relieved, and I went a bit further. I told her she was very worried, but she shouldn't be. I also told her not to feel alone because there are many people there for her and I told her a few other things the souls gave me which I cannot remember now. She confirmed what I told her. I asked her if I could give her my card and she said yes. I let her know I wasn't looking for anything, but I was just giving her that message. The woman who came to me turned out to be her Godmother. There was a lot of emotion coming from her Godmother and it was making me tear up.

She told me she was just speaking to her Godmother on the drive over asking her to give her a sign that things would be okay in court and I was there to reassure her that her Godmother was there, and all will be well. We ended our conversation. It felt very awkward. I don't know if she will be in touch again, but that was a first for me. I pray that things went well for her---as well as her Godmother told me it would.

The Unexpected Visitor

I was working at the Practical Magik Store in Sugarloaf NY one today when Pat quickly walked in somewhat excited. She announced to Denise, the owner, and I that she was driving by when she saw the store. Pat told us she didn't know why but she just had to come in. She saw the crystals and felt it was the reason she came in.

As I stood there watching Denise and Pat choose some crystals, I had an older woman come to me that I figured she must be Pat's mother or grandmother. Because I don't just walk up to strangers and start a session, I didn't say anything to Pat but this soul was now telling me she's Pat's grandmother and she wouldn't leave me alone. I strongly feel it's completely unethical to just approach someone not looking for a session and start giving them messages from the other side so I didn't say anything.

As Pat was paying for the crystals, the soul who is with me the whole time kept bugging me to say something before Pat left but I refused to do so. Suddenly Pat said, "I feel I need something else." She turned, went back to the crystals, and told us that she wasn't sure what to get. This was my opening. I told her to pick something pink that will help her bring back her passion. She looked at me and asked how I knew that. I told her that her grandmother is with me and is telling me you have lost your passion. It was at that point Denise told her who I was. Pat smiled and said, "maybe that is why I felt had to come in when I saw the store." I for sure had no doubt about that.

Outwardly, I would have thought that she was full of life and a happy person. However, I hear messages telling me what is down deep below the surface. Pat went back to looking at the crystals. Not being a "new age" guy, I had no idea what she should get because I truly don't know one crystal from the next; however, I was staring at some pink and white stones. She just happened to pick out three of them. She then looked at me and she decided that she had some time for a session.

It turned out it was her grandmother who was with me; a few others came through with strong messages about her passion for life. The messages were healing and about how she could fix the one thing that wasn't working in her life. Pat felt lonely and that life was just passing her by. The souls told Pat it was her perception and that she needed to look closer at how people in her life she felt weren't there, are there for her.

This isn't the first time I have encountered someone who has come into the Practical Magik store in Sugar Loaf, saying they don't know why they are there. Ultimately, they wind up having an important session with me that helped them on their journey in this life.

Nothing that happens to me surprises me anymore. To all my clients from Practical Magik and beyond, thank you all for your support, you are the reason I was granted my gifts.

Neil The Security Guard

Upon arriving at 1 Wall Street in Manhattan where I was on assignment for a video project, I arrived at the site a little early, and no one was at site safety where I check in. One of the security guards, Neil, escorted me into the building and up to site safety where I signed in.

As Neil and I stepped into the elevator, a big man from the other side was with me. The soul kept saying, "talk to my boy." He wanted me to tell Neil he was here with us. I told this soul it wasn't a good idea. Neil and I don't know each other, and he saw me as a photographer there to shoot a video. What if Neil wasn't receptive, plus, this is a job where I am representing another company. I need to use discretion. I didn't let Neil know this man was with me.

This soul was persistent while I was shooting alone on the floors. The soul who now identified himself as Neil's dad kept coming back to me telling me again to "speak to his boy." Again, I refused and continued about my business. I thought that was it finally. Nope.

As I was leaving the job, I was just about through the gate when bam; this soul is with me again, "talk to my boy." I told the soul, okay, I'll see how this goes, and it better go well. This man laughed and said, "Not to worry."

I came back to Neil and asked him, "did your dad pass and was he a big man with a deep voice?" Before he could answer, I told him what I did and asked him if it would be okay hearing from who I believed was his dad. His dad told me the character was important to him (Neil) and it always was, even as a little boy. I told him he could have gone down a bad path in life but stopped and chose the path of self-respect. He just looked at me and again I apologized for doing this to him.

I asked if this was his dad, as I believed he may be. I told him he this man with me was an influence for him growing up. He said no, he wasn't but knows who he is. Neil told me it was his uncle who he was named after, and that my description fit him perfectly. His uncle who took the place of his dad who he never knew and was his dad from his point of view.

Neil pulled up his sleeve showing me the hair stand up on his arm was standing up. Neil advised me, "what you said made perfect sense; you nailed it."

I gave him my card and told him to call me. He told me he will definitely reach out. I ended up going down once more and saw Neil, and this time his mother came through. I filled Neil in on what else I was getting of which I have little recollection as usual. The souls speak through me and I let it go. Neil never reached out again. I surely hope one day he will.

I really hate doing that to people and when I do, I cannot and will not charge them; it's an ethical thing. I don't believe it's right to blindside someone and then charge them. I guess it's time for me to stop setting boundaries for myself; well actually the souls will not stay within them anyway.

My Interview on Talk with TQ

I was invited to be on a local TV talk show with Toni Quest. I never give messages on shows I'm on and this one was no different. We simply talked about what I do. However, as I was being miked for sound by the producer, James, he said to me, "Don't get anyone for me." I said, "no problem," even though I was getting something. I never just give people messages out of the blue. It really is, in my opinion, unethical and I understand that not everyone is into this.

He laughed and said, "No it's okay. If anyone comes in let me know." My reply was, "Good because your mother is here." I described the woman and he confirmed it was his mother who had passed. I told him she was telling me he needed to have confidence in his work and to be kind and not be so hard on himself, and much more. His sound guy laughed and said, "That is so right on." A woman there who was the photographer doing camera work on the show, said the same thing.

Now for you skeptics, I didn't know James was going to be there or there was a crew or who would be on the crew. I have known Toni for many years. She invited me to come on her show to speak about what my gifts are all about.

So, there was no way I could have Googled James nor would I. However, I know, if I did, the messages that I got for him would not have come up in any search. I don't read people's Facebook pages or anything else because it may be all made up and not true. If someone who calls themselves a psychic / medium has to do that, they aren't real, and it will come out.

The show runs about 30 minutes. If you would like to watch it, it is on Toni's YouTube where she posts the show after they run. Mine ran for three weeks. Enjoy it.

Remaining Grateful for My Gifts...Always

Honesty is unwavering and an important part of who I am. Throughout my life, I give it my all and I do my very best with everything I do. Knowing this I still push myself further to improve and go beyond my own expectations. As a self-taught award-winning photographer, that works well for me. I never become complacent. I never feel that I am the best photographer out there.

I carry that into my sessions as well, and I always want more for my client. It's very important for me to know they get the messages they need at that time. I pray every day for these gifts to get stronger and they do. As of this writing, I have always received messages for the person with me and I have never had to tell anyone I couldn't get messages for them. Even the skeptics and atheists, get messages from me. One woman, Sheryl, couldn't identify the souls that were with me, so I just went into the messages they were giving. She totally related to the messages she was getting. I was told later by someone who knew Sheryl that she was amazed because she had been to five mediums and none of them could "read" her. Some of them told her that she had the gifts, and that was why they couldn't get anything for her. She asked me if I saw that in her and I told her, "No, I didn't see that."

I question myself and push myself to be better for my clients. I do know it's not me but rather the divine spirits who grant me these gifts and the souls who come to talk to me. I also know we can only hear the messages the souls feel are important to my clients at the time of the session. I get it, but I always want more. I walk away from every session wondering and hoping my client heard what they needed to hear.

I was working in a store at Sugar Loaf. A Tarot reader was right next to me There was only a cloth curtain separating us. It zapped my energy. I had to struggle to keep my energy up. I couldn't believe this was happening to me. In the time between my clients, I heard some of what she was telling people. I was shocked anyone would believe what they were being told. I couldn't believe they thought it was coming from the cards and not what they were telling the card reader, during a conversation. I don't want to slam her, and I will not, but all I'll say is that I realized she wasn't legitimate. It did, however, get me wondering. Are my messages that way? I knew the difference was she engaged people in conversations and she asked a lot of questions. I don't.

My messages are very different. As I sat questioning this, praying for more and stronger gifts I went on my Facebook page. There was a message in my inbox that couldn't have been timelier. It was something I really needed to know at the time. Now question this if you must, but I met with Andrea a year prior to her sending me this. Think about that for a minute. The souls knew I had to hear something to keep the faith in myself and in them as a renewal and here it is:

"Hi, Bob, We met last year. You came to my condo when I was pregnant. What I never told you and I've been meaning

to, was that I haven't had the need to find another medium or psychic for more answers because what we talked about and what you shared was enough. That has never happened to me before and I know you're the real deal and I thank you. Also, more importantly, what really sealed the deal was that you told me my stepfather (who was in the car with me) had a message and he was yelling "look to the right' and I had no idea what you were talking about. WELL, later that day I remembered that I started taking a new way to work, and at one point on the Bronx River Parkway, near the dam, you have to merge into traffic in a really precarious circle. That very day that we met I was merging and I thought there were no cars and as I went into the right lane a speeding truck was upon me. Sammy was yelling look to the right. It all made sense. You're awesome and I hope we can meet again for another session. Thank you, Andrea"

I asked her if it was all right to use what she said but use a different name. She told me it was okay and to feel free to use her name if I wanted to. I wasn't going to use her name but I felt it gave more validity to this, so I did use her real name, but I left off her last name for obvious reasons.

Before anyone tells me that I must have more confidence in myself, just know I have confidence in the souls and in the divine spirits. Once we become overconfident and make this about ourselves, our gifts diminish or leave totally. So, I will continue to question and push myself, to do better. I am who I am and who I will always be. I will continue to pray before each session, and I know the souls and messages will come. Thank you, Andrea, for this message. Thank you also to everyone who has ever written a testimonial on my website, thanked me in a text, or personally messaged me on Facebook.

Most of all, thank you God and all the divine spirits for granting me these gifts.

Chapter Eight
Galleries

A Gallery is when a group of people sit together in the same room. I try to get something for everyone, and so far, it's how it has worked out.

The messages I get are not as in-depth as a private session. They are good, don't get me wrong, just not as in-depth, because I am moving around the room trying to get something for everyone. When I start, I ask anyone who would just like to observe and not receive messages to please let me know because I try to get something for everyone and I don't want to take time away from the others.

Lions Club Psychic Fair, Aromas, and Moving Objects And The Events That Surrounded It

My gifts are growing and becoming stronger which recently has included the aroma of food, smoke, and various other things during my sessions with my clients. For example, I was doing a session with Jane and Mary, her sister, in New Jersey when suddenly I smelled apple pie which came for only a second or two. I was able to see the kitchen from where we were sitting, and nothing was cooking or baking at the time. I had been there about an hour at this point, and I knew there was no apple pie anywhere. I asked my client Jane if she and her sister Mary, who was sitting with her, smelled it. They told me, no, but they both started to laugh. Their mother showed me a very large apple pie. When I advised them what I was seeing they told me their mother who was with us on the other side, made apple pies all the time. Their mother made one for a special occasion that was very large, but it fell off the seat of the car and broke.

At another session, there was the smell of a pork roast. It was during a session at a pizzeria. I knew that pizza places do not make pork roasts but asked the owner anyway. I was told no, nothing like that was cooking. It was my client Gina's mother who made that for special occasions. When I smell something it's often what the soul made for special occasions

I did sessions at a Charity Fair for a Lions club in Montrose, NY. At the time, I had yet to do a gallery session. I was under the assumption I was doing private sessions for them, but to my surprise, I was set up to do a Gallery. It was at night in a high school room and the chairs were set up in a circle. There were ten or eleven women with me in the room. In the middle of the circle was an empty water bottle lying on its side along with a lollipop wrapper. I should have picked it up, but I didn't; however, there was a reason for this that became clear during the session.

The bottle was pointing north next to the lollipop wrapper. While I was going around the circle giving the participants messages, my attention was brought to my right. I looked over at four women sitting there. I had a grandfather with me, but I wasn't sure who he was there for. Then it happened. My eyes were guided to the bottle. The bottle had moved to the right and it pointed southeast right toward a young woman whose Grandfather had just passed. He was present for her in the room. I looked at the bottle than the woman, and again back and forth three times to make sure it was for her. I was reassured it was. I asked her if her Grandfather had passed and she acknowledged that he had. It turned out this man had another granddaughter and daughter in the room as well whom I had already given messages. He was concerned I would pass over his other granddaughter so that is why he moved the bottle to point right at her. Souls don't let me know they have others in the room until after the session is finished. This happens all the time to me, so the message is fresh for the one they want to talk to.

For the record, there was no one even close to the bottle and no heavy winds in the room. It could not have moved by itself.

After I finished her session I stopped and said I thought the bottle was in the center of the room. I asked if anyone saw it move. A woman to my left told me she saw it move. The grandfather had clearly moved it. One more thing that came out of this event:

About a week later I received an e-mail from someone who couldn't get to the Fair where she had booked a session. At the end of our session she told me she looked at all the mediums listed for the event, and they kept bringing her back to my profile. After the third time, she gave up trying to read all the others and settled on me. This validates what I have been told by my souls--- that it is the relatives from the other side who bring my clients to me. The souls tell me this all the time. Now I can believe them and thank the souls for having faith in me. I am also thankful every day for my gifts and for my being able to help others through the prompting of the souls. The gifts they have given me are healing gifts.

I would like to send out my appreciation also to those of you who have come to meet with me. It is a privilege that I am so thankful for. So, a big 'Thank You' goes out to all of you.

The Birthday Party

There were nine women at what turned out to be a birthday party. This was my very first gallery. I had no idea it was going to be a birthday celebration. I worried that I wouldn't get anything at all because I don't want to let anyone down. It is very important to me. Paulette was the person who set this up. She had a grandfather that crossed over. He was with me for two days prior to our session. Even with him coming through I worried I wouldn't get messages for the other attendees. I prayed hard that they would.

Once in the car and on my way, the souls started to come in. I got the soul of a father coming through to me. This Soul was strong; also, I had a nurse and a hairdresser with me.

Once the sessions started and I went into my routine that brings the souls through, the father that was with me on my way over was with me. I looked right at the Birthday girl Joann and told her her dad was with us. I didn't even have to ask for validation that he had passed because he was a solid soul and she began to cry. This session went very well. I had no idea, but Joann was the one I was there for and all the others hoped that he would come through for her.

As I continued with the sessions after the birthday girl's dad had come through for her other messages and the souls started to really come through. As it turned out everyone there that night received messages.

However, this is what also happened. The homeowner Amy had a dog. I close my eyes when I give messages, but I heard Amy say she would put the dog in another room. With that everyone yelled at her not to. I didn't know why. Because I am seeing the visions when I'm getting the messages, I see very little that is going on around me. I hadn't noticed anything. What was happening was the dog would go and sit in front of the person about to receive the message. This occurred with everyone who was about to get messages. The dog seemed to sense it and did this every time as I was about to get messages for them. The hairdresser Lisa had her Grandmother come. Her Grandmother was the one who came to me on the ride over. The granddaughter was in a great deal of emotional pain. The dog actually licked her hand and I knew it was a kiss from her Grandmother letting her know she is still looking out over her.

The other interesting thing that occurred during this party was a penny dropped out of nowhere between Paulette and Jessica whose friend had died in a car crash. They had no idea where it came from or why, so I asked the souls to tell me. The woman who passed in the auto accident came back to tell me Jessica loaned her money and wanted to pay her back. I asked

Jessica whose friend passed in a car accident if she loaned her money and if the woman never or rarely paid her back. She confirmed it; I told her she just paid you back. She looked at me and laughingly said, "A penny really?" I replied, "What can I tell you?" It was a fun exchange that showed Jessica her friend still had a sense of humor on the other side! It came to me the next day that Jessica's friend wanted her to know that she is in heaven, so she dropped a penny.

"Pennies from Heaven" was a great message for both of us and this is why I do this work.

Footnote: I asked Paulette days later if that penny was heads up as I saw it. She told me yes. I don't know why I didn't say it that night; it was what the souls showed me. You can read about this in Paulette's testimonial below:

"So, Saturday night I asked Bob to do a Gallery session for my friends Bday Party. Apparently, my grandfather was with him for 2 days, I imagine like people line up a sale 24hrs before Black Friday making sure he got his turn lol. Bob nailed EVERYONE! It was amazing! The host's dog went to each person Bob was reading WHILE he was reading them. But what got me the most was during the readings me and a friend heard a coin hit the floor. Later when we looked, a penny was on the floor right between us. It wasn't hers, it wasn't mine, the table we were sitting next to had a lip on it so there's no way it fell off the table. It just appeared. Literally OUT OF THIN AIR. When we asked Bob about it he asked my friend if the person who came through for her owed her money, she said yes and he thought it was that. He just told me tonight that he figured it out. Asking if she owed money was to validate it was for my friend and not me, but it was a "penny from heaven" to let her know her friend was in heaven! It was an amazing experience and will definitely have him do a party again as well as private readings!"
- Paulette, Carmel, NY

Helen

I met Helen at another Gallery. As always, I asked anyone who would just like to observe and not receive messages to please let me know because I try to get something for everyone and I don't want to take time away from the others.

I had the soul of a woman coming through for someone. This soul gave me messages about her life which she validated. When I asked the woman, Helen, receiving the messages if it sounded like it was her friend which was what I was hearing, Helen's response was, "but the soul could be any one of a number of people." She then went on to advise me she is a scientist and wanted more proof. I do get crossover in these situations, so I advised her that I can only give you what the souls give me and want you to hear. I then asked if the messages made sense for anyone else, but they didn't. Suddenly, I heard the name Annie from the soul. She said it five times. Now, names aren't something I get often and because this woman was so difficult I was resisting saying the name. Yes, she was that difficult, but the fifth time the soul said it, she insisted I say it, so I did. The woman said to me, "no the name means nothing."

The man next to her said he had a friend who passed with that name. I said it was unlikely because it came from the soul who was with me for the scientist. I then moved onto the next person and started messages for her. When Helen said, "wait the name does mean something to me." As it turned out the soul had a horse she was fond of, and Annie was the name of her horse.

This is what I mean by depth. Had it been a private session, the horse most likely would have come through right away and left no doubt about who the soul was. I only get short messages, because everyone who attends a gallery has messages that are important coming from the souls around them. If I get stuck in the minor details like I get during full sessions, the important messages would be lost. This particular soul felt everything she had given me in the situation should have been enough, however, when it wasn't she showed me the horse.

I just completed my first two public galleries where I knew absolutely no one there. The women who produced them told everyone who booked not to tell them anything as to why they wanted to come. They didn't want there to be any question that the message I was getting was coming directly from the other side. I wouldn't be able to remember what I was told anyway, and there was no assigned seating. I don't have long hair where I can hide an earpiece and there were no microphones around. For me, this must be upfront and real. Both went well, from what I was told by the attendees and the feedback the producers got afterward.

I would like to thank both the producers Lisa & Sabrina.

The Souls Only Guide Us

Many don't understand how the other side works. We are often under the impression the souls will do things for us. Some believe that so much they seek out the souls far too often.

The souls are there to guide us; they simply can't do things for us. Do they open and close doors? Absolutely. Do the souls push you through it? No. You have to move through the door on your own.

They want what is best for us, however, we have free will and can reject their guidance. Many of us do not understand the connection to the other side and look at things that happen as coincidences, but there are no coincidences. One doesn't need to continuously look for these connections; just live your life with the confidence they are there for you.

We need to have faith in both the souls and the divine spirits as they will never let us down. We need to live our lives and do the best we can in this life, trusting we do have guidance. Trust this. Do not continue to reach out to them for every little thing, and don't keep looking for validation moving from one medium to another. If you don't trust them they will stop coming to you through those here on earth who can hear them. It takes a lot of their energy to come through, so if you look at it this way you will understand what I am saying. When you are being taught something, you know what it is you have to do. If you go from teacher to teacher or keep asking the teacher the same questions, they get tired of giving you validation and feel you are using up their time. They have to move onto things you don't know or on to teach others who also need them. If you are in a bad place they have no issue coming through for you to lift you toward that journey of healing; just don't keep going to them to help you find your keys or a mate. This isn't why they come through, to me anyway.

Have faith in them, but most of all have faith in yourself.

He Gifted Me Tomatoes

One of my clients called to set up a small gallery with her and perhaps four others. There was a possibility that her husband might sit in. However, this was primarily for her mother-in-law.

Upon my arrival, I was introduced to everyone. Her husband, let's call him John, was giving me looks. I could feel them go right through me. He was skeptical; hell, he downright had no belief in what I do. He seemed ready to expose me as a fraud and he thought I was just there to grab his hard-earned money.

As it turned out there were only three of us. The mother in law, my client and her husband who asked me immediately upon being introduced, if there was money buried in the basement of the family home. This is not usually what I tend to do but okay, I'll see what the souls will tell me, if anything, I told him.

So here is the scene. His mom is on my left and he is way over on my right with his wife. He was waiting to pounce. His father comes through fast filling me in on who he was. As I am giving the mother the messages from her husband and a few other souls who came through, John's father brings my attention to his son. I look over to see John's head turned away from everyone. His father, a prankster, chuckled and said he is a skeptic no more.

During his messages, the first thing I said to John was, "You found money in a can in the basement." He confirmed that he had found a can filled with silver coins. It went on from there. I saw this tough, non-believer, or at the very least strong skeptic, became emotional. By the way, this is a common occurrence. When John realized the messages were true, he was no longer skeptical.

Back to the buried money--I saw a patch with cracks in the floor of the basement of the family home. I told John about what I saw. He confirmed there was such a patch. I drew him a picture of the vision, which was the first time and last time I have ever done that. I didn't hear from him, so I doubt the money was there. As it turned out this was not a surprise because it was confirmed by everyone sitting in the room with me that John's father was a prankster while here, and he continued that behavior during the session.

I don't do these sessions to try and find wallets or keys (Hell, I can't even find mine sometimes!). I bring messages of what you need to do to move through your life. I don't do what I call parlor tricks. No. It's about you and their plan to help you move on.

Everyone was happy with the messages at the end and as I left, everyone, including John, thanked me for the messages. Just as I was starting to pull out of his driveway, John runs out with a bag and asks me if I like tomatoes. I tell him that I do. He hands me the bag containing fresh tomatoes he grew himself in his garden. His gesture meant a lot to me as I knew it was his way of saying thank you again and showing me his appreciation for what occurred during the session. He wanted me to have something he spent so much time growing and nurturing, a part of himself.

I knew exactly what I was going to do with them. As a kid, we had gardens in the back of our apartments. We grew our own tomatoes and often made tomato sandwiches.

John brought back fond childhood memories long forgotten. Thank you, John, for the memories and a delicious tomato sandwich.

Chapter Nine
Lessons Learned, Lessons Shared

As a Caulbearer, I know the souls want us to honor them. They always tell me that. On one Father's Day, I realized it is a wonderful time to honor the fathers who are living and those who have passed. I posted this on my Facebook medium/Caulbearer page about dads but it applies to moms too.

On Father's Day, Mother's Day, or on any day for that matter, you should let mom or dad know how much you appreciate what they do for you. If they have passed, smile and fondly remember the time you spent with them. If they have passed, say a prayer to them. Say hello and let them know your thoughts are with them. Celebrate them and the time spent here with you. It is an honor to them when you celebrate them and when you appreciate their time here with you. You also should keep them fondly in your hearts. And please don't wear their passing on your sleeve. Believe me, they are around you and they will hear and see you.

Honor them by celebrating their life and not their passing. This is what the souls want us all to do. It is what I do for both my mom and dad. I always have them in my heart not on my sleeve as some people do.

We travel through our life thinking our loved ones will be here forever and then one day they may leave us and journey home, or perhaps simply move away. Some of us rarely take the time to appreciate them. We may get upset with each other (often over petty things) and we think we will eventually make up, but then something may happen, and we will never get the chance to forgive or apologize. They may leave before we can have that opportunity.

Unless a parent or someone else in your life is not a good person, and it does occasionally happen, you should always treat them and others in your life as if it were their last day here. Live every day as if it is your last.

I am always learning about myself and my gifts. As I have often said these gifts are given to me by God and they are not to be taken for granted. I never do.

I did a small party and the messages flowed well. I was happy with the way they went and if you know me, that is unusual. I always want the souls to give me more, even though I know I can only hear what they intend for me to hear.

At the end of a party after all the messages were delivered, I did something I never do. I had a bite to eat with my host and some of the others. I asked the host how she found me. She explained that a friend of theirs was with me at a party. I had a hard time remembering her at first, not unusual and nothing personal. I cannot remember most of what I tell my clients, as the messages come through me from the souls. They told me their friend was told by me that her husband didn't die the way she was told. What happens sometimes, the "movie", (visions) as I call it, plays, and the movie showed me what actually happened. This only happens when a soul has a point to make.

What played in the movie was going against the official report. I told her he didn't die in the building as the accident report stated, but went outside and hit his head on a car when he fell. My response when they reminded me what I said was, "I told her that?" They said I had and that I was accurate. I asked how their friend found this out. Well, she found out there were cameras in the area and the videos showed exactly what I saw. I was floored; here I am going against everything real up to that point, meaning, police reports, etc., and it turned out the message I got was right. I was shocked but realized more than ever I must

94

trust what the movie the souls show me. Yes, this has happened before, but I rarely get confirmation like this.

A strange thing happened when I inquired how they found me. The host advised me that their friend did not have my phone number, so she googled me. She told me she found my web page (the only one I have) and saw my number at the bottom of the page. My phone number has NEVER been on my site anywhere. The only phone number on my site is to the store in Sugar Loaf I work at to book appointments. She swears up and down that's where she got it. Before I wrote this, I looked everywhere on the site and no, my number isn't on there. Stranger things have happened, but I'm glad the souls who brought me to them, put my number on there for her to find. I am sure it was her father who came through for her.

I am blessed with this gift as painful as it often is. I consider myself blessed and thank God and the divine spirits for granting me these gifts.

Please know that everything you have read is not about me. The messages simply come through me. I'm just the vehicle who has been chosen by God to receive the gifts that enable me to hear the souls. It is God and the divine spirits who open the skylight in Heaven in order for me to see and hear messages for my clients. This is about your loved ones who send messages to me so I can, in turn, relay these messages to my clients, helping them to journey toward a better life and guide them towards healing.

It is only now that I understand why my journey in life has been what it is; why I always want to help others and why the experiences I have had and the hardships I have suffered were so much a part of my life. My path was all in preparation for me to do this and to endure the pain that comes along with it. This is my destiny. It is the greater plan God has for me and I am honored to be granted this gift that enables me to serve others.

If I or anyone else makes this about themselves or about money, they have no understanding of what this is all about. If that happens, the gifts are taken away. I have no intention of sacrificing my gift by making this about me or about greed.

I hope you enjoyed this book and that you have a greater understanding of how this all works.

God bless and remain strong.
- Bob Buchanan
Caulbearer

Glossary

Galleries – when a gathering of more than two people sit together in the same room to receive messages.

Sessions – others call these reading. I refere to them as sessions.

Souls – spirit or spirit guides. I prefer Souls over Spirit.

Movie – visions I have.

Caul – the veil.

Caulbearer – a person who is born with a veil.

About The Author

Born with a veil on his face, a sign of psychic abilities, Bob understood from a very early age he was different. At the age of 8 Bob began to see strong visions of the future and of things to come. Not understanding exactly what was happening, Bob ignored them, thinking it was simply his imagination. As he grew older they were more timely. He knew within a half hour when something was going to happen, but continued to ignore the messages until recently, when he began to receive strong messages and visions from beyond for others.

Bob receives calls worldwide, as well as all from over the country and Canada. His clients come to him almost exclusively through referrals. Loved ones or souls for others come from beyond to Bob no matter where he is. Bob will tell you that the messages come for people sitting next to him or walking by. "I never know when they will come, they just find me."

When bob does a session, he always gets messages from beyond that are positive. Bob never asks his client questions, nor will he allow them to give him any information until it's established who is coming through and why they are here.

The messages are uplifting and healing for those receiving them. Bob considers himself a healer as much as a Caulbearer. He is thankful for his gifts which allow him to help others in a time of need.

Contact: 914.879.1115
Bbucha3458@aol.com

CPSIA information can be obtained
at www.ICGtesting.com
Printed in the USA
BVOW08s1715220118
505883BV00001B/1/P